INCOME DETERMINATION
IN THE INTERNATIONAL PETROLEUM INDUSTRY

Abdulhadi Hassan Taher

Former Governor-General, Petroleum & Mineral Organization
Managing Director, Saudi Arabian Fertilizer Co., Saudi Arabia
Lecturer in Business Administration, Riyadh University
Aramco Board Member 1965–1986

Income Determination
in the International Petroleum Industry

SAQI

London San Francisco Beirut

ISBN: 978-0-86356-632-5

First published by Pergamon Press, New York, 1966
This edition published by Saqi, London, 2008

© Abdulhadi Hassan Taher, 2008

A full CIP record for this book is available from the British Library.
A full CIP record for this book is available from the Library of Congress.

Manufactured in Lebanon

SAQI
26 Westbourne Grove, London W2 5RH
825 Page Street, Suite 203, Berkeley, California 94710
Tabet Building, Mneimneh Street, Hamra, Beirut
www.saqibooks.com

Contents

Contents

Contents

Introduction

by Maurice Moonitz
Professor of Accounting, University of California, Berkeley

THE ACCOUNTING problems of the petroleum industry have withstood a satisfactory solution for many decades. The uncertainties associated with exploration for oil deposits make it difficult to account adequately for the heavy outlays necessary to find the oil. The development of a discovered field is less uncertain only by a matter of degree, because the actual extent of the deposit cannot be known accurately in advance. The processing of the oil in a refinery involves the use of known quantities of a basic raw material, but crude oil is a complex hydrocarbon which also contains chemical impurities of different sorts. As a result several joint products emerge from the one basic raw material, and the awesome problem of allocating joint costs in some rational manner has to be faced. Add to these technical problems the social and political issues created by the international operation of many large oil companies and it becomes easy to see why the accounting problems have withstood satisfactory solution for so long.

The present study injects a fresh point of view into the problem. It does so by refusing to be bound by the customary limits of past discussions of the same type of problem. At the broadest level, Dr. Taher has brought into play some of the techniques and methods of the social sciences generally, especially that part of social science that has emerged recently under the title of "organization theory". In particular, he makes the "petroleum organization" his focus, viewing it as a kind of organism operating in an environment which is partly hostile or at least not ideally suited for the one essential goal of any organism, namely, its survival. By this method, he is able to identify the various parties interested in "the petroleum organization" – e.g. creditors, shareholders, employees, taxing authorities, and the governments both of the host country and the home country – and to describe the kinds of pressures and stresses they create in the organization.

In a nutshell, he can describe the bias that any one group has in the results of the activities of the organization.

Having described the biases, Dr. Taher then is in a position to determine the response of the organization, especially with respect to the key accounting issue of income determination. He concludes that instead of a series of special, tailor-made calculations, one for each pressure group, the organization is best served by preparing and disseminating the results of an objective determination, what he calls the "neutral value of net income".

An integral part of any study of accounting in the petroleum industry is the treatment of joint costs. Dr. Taher deals with joint costs on at least two fronts: the problem of "transfer prices" from one division of an international petroleum organization to another division as an essential element in determining the revenues to be assigned to each, and the problem of allocating costs between crude oil and natural gas as an essential element in determining the expenses incurred in producing each. Again, he follows a method that is typical of his broad orientation; he looks to the chemistry of hydrocarbons to supply the firm, factual foundation on the basis of which he can then erect a formal system of cost allocation to solve the accounting problem.

This study is a welcome addition to the literature because it deals with a related set of real problems, problems that are with us today and will remain in the foreseeable future, and also because it does not shrink from using the best available tools in the social sciences to propose a solution to those problems. I hope that we have more studies like this one, both from Dr. Taher and from others who will employ the same broad, solidly-based methods that he has.

M. Moonitz
Berkeley, California

Foreword

THE ACTIVITIES necessary for delivering petroleum and its derivatives to consumers are performed by a complex system of international trading and processing organizations which deal with each other as well as with various governments. This dissertation pays special attention to the financial aspects of the production and export of petroleum because they are of critical importance within the system.

The techniques presently employed to measure the revenues, expenses, assets and liabilities (the basic determinants of net income and of rate of return) of these organizations are not sufficiently objective. Yet a more objective system of measurement can be achieved within the framework of currently available techniques.

In order to achieve this more objective system, an organization model is constructed to simulate an oil company in the international petroleum industry. Survival and security are postulated as the organization's dominating goals. To achieve these goals the organization must keep certain critical variables within assigned limits. These variables interact with a set of environmental factors or disturbances. Since an organization's survival depends, among other things, on the realization of profits, the determination of its periodic net income is of crucial importance. As a consequence, a theory of the "neutral value of net income" is constructed on the basis of the exercise of a rational choice among the accounting and other techniques available at the present time for the measurement of net income. The criteria of choice are those previously developed in the organizational model. The conclusion is reached that the basic goals of the organization will be served best by an unbiased determination of income.

The findings of the study are then applied to published accounting and other data for this industry, with estimates employed to fill in the gaps. The amounts of periodic net income and the related rates of return determined by this application differ substantially from those actually reported by the industry.

Abdulhadi H. Taher
Berkeley, California

CHAPTER I
———

Orientation and Introduction

1.1. The Problem

THIS BOOK is an investigation and evaluation of some of the important aspects of accounting theory and practices in the international petroleum industry. The reason underlying this choice is the great significance of the accounting data and the accounting methodology in relations between an oil company and an oil exporting government, among the oil exporting countries themselves, and between the exporting countries represented by the Organization of Petroleum Exporting Countries and the oil companies individually and as an informal group. Furthermore, the same data will be of critical importance in relations between the exporting countries and the petroleum consuming countries, should a discussion of petroleum pricing take place. Our purpose in this study is to delineate a more satisfactory methodology within the conventional framework of accounting theory for the particular needs of an international petroleum organization, for we have found that the accounting techniques used by the international petroleum industry today are inadequate to supply fundamental and unbiased information to the decision-makers in the oil companies and in the exporting and consuming governments. Our method of deriving these more satisfactory techniques is eclectic, drawing from sources both within and without the body of conventional accounting material, for we feel that no one set of accounting techniques can adequately serve all the purposes of the petroleum industry.

The approach of choosing a certain industry for examination of accounting theory should not be misunderstood. It is only because in accounting applications abstract theory must be supplemented with practical evidence to satisfactorily serve business decision-makers. We shall offer practical techniques supported by sound theories, theories which are defensible within a given acceptable frame of reference. The rules of logic and consistency should dominate the construction of such theories, but the soundness of these theories should prove evident through the testing in an empirical and practical situation.

Our pilot plant in this book is the international petroleum industry. The structure of the pilot plant will be drawn in the form of an organizational model. Then tests will be made and results enumerated. We do not offer a case study, but rather a conceptual fabric which combines and describes the pressures and the goals of the oil companies and the petroleum exporting and consuming countries. Such an approach should be very useful to both the academician and the oil businessman or government administrator. It provides the accounting analyst with a framework that combines the virtues of being relatively more objective and demonstrably applicable, in a practical situation.

Further, we believe that the practical techniques we shall offer can open new areas for utilizing the benefits accounting can provide. Under our analytical methods, concern with principles or standards is replaced by emphasis on means and ends, on the use of cognitively rational decisions in choosing the means which are most satisfactory in achieving the desired ends.

1.2. Science and the Businessman's Problems

The decision-maker, in business and in government, must at times face problems that are too difficult to solve. Yet he must choose one course of action against another. His judgment and his experience fail to guide him fully in such situations. Of course, there are some business problems which do not lend themselves to scientific treatment but almost all of them can be made simpler, if not wholly solved, through techniques commonly used in scientific disciplines. Choosing one accounting method against the other can, under the set of circumstances which prevails in the international petroleum industry, belong to the category of problems where application of the rules of cognitively rational choice used in some disciplines is most useful. In this industry, when faced with the problem of choosing an accounting method, the manager will rely on his controllers and the company auditors. The controller has little choice; he will rely on what are called "generally accepted accounting principles". However, if it is a managerial question, he does have the freedom of deriving a solution by applying his accounting judgment to it, even though he may lack a sufficiently definite system to work with. In order to test a solution in a more objective manner, we should be able to depict the organization as a whole and test the effects and consequences of the decision on the viability and existence of the organization. Although the facilities for such a procedure are rarely at his disposal, the manager should proceed in this manner. He should work within a dynamic aggregative system, rather than within a particular stationary system.

Usually, however, the accountant limits himself to the particular stationary analysis. He examines his problem most frequently as if the accounting methods and data were prepared in a vacuum. Although many industrial accountants attempt to serve their management by preparing analytical accounting statements, they rarely, if ever, take into consideration factors outside the immediate management requirement.

Our purpose in this study, then, is to derive an organizational model compatible with contemporary organization theories and to describe the integral part that accounting data and methodology play in such a model. We shall try to show that there is a fundamental unity in the fields of business administration; that, although they are named differently, they belong essentially to one system; and that they function as sub-systems of the organization system. We cannot treat accounting as a separate field of knowledge, because all functions of business administration are related to each other and react and affect each other in many different and known ways. The result of their aggregate reactions and complex relationships and interactions determines the failure or success of the organization. There are degrees of success and failure which are the results of business decisions, of which accounting decisions are only one set. Personnel decisions, inventory control decisions, marketing decisions, and any departmental decision could affect the ultimate success or failure of the organization's efforts. The unity among all these so-called separate fields of knowledge is two fold, both in its effect on the results of composite organization behavior and through the interrelation and interaction of these several fields in its effect upon decisions of the organization. Although in this book we will be concerned only with accounting, we shall attempt to join accounting theory and practice with organization theory.

In an editorial note in *Cybernetics and Management*, H. Pennycuick writes:

> This belief, that the voice of experience – or flair – will solve all business problems is no more justified than the opposite view that any business problem can be solved by scientific means. What is true, however, is that there are very few difficult business problems that cannot to some extent be lightened by scientific treatment.[1]

The necessity of choosing accounting principles, concepts or methods to be used in a business situation is a fundamental problem of the decision-maker and, in this instance, we find that Pennycuick's opinion is particularly applicable. If the application of scientific methodology will not solve the complex problems encountered in the business world, the use of these techniques will at least contribute to a relatively more satisfactory solution.

1.3 Accounting Aims and Methods

We believe that it is useful to both the accountant and to business management to treat accounting in a more rational manner, for thus it will serve their aims better and will enable them to arrive at more satisfactory decisions. We agree that accounting is a management tool, and we further believe and shall demonstrate that the basic objective of a business organization is security and survival. Accounting can serve this goal by communicating to the organization, objective and unbiased reports of its environment and its position in that environment. It can give the organization the information with which to act on those factors upon which its security and survival are based.

In *Models of Man*, Herbert Simon says that

> A theory of administration or of organization cannot exist without a theory of rational choice.[2]

This viewpoint is adopted throughout in this study. It is a part of our logical

---

1. Stafford Beer, *Cybernetics and Management* (London: The English Universities Press, 1960), p. 1.
2. Herbert A. Simon, *Models of Man, Social and Rational* (New York: John Wiley, 1957), p. 196.

system of treating accounting theory and methodology. We are still in the same arena where the belief that "there is every reason to think that the revolutionary possibilities of science extend immeasurably beyond what has so far been realized"[1] dominates.

1.3. A. Accounting as a Social Science

For our purpose, we shall define accounting as a part of social sciences. Because it deals, directly or indirectly, not only with events but also with human desires and judgments as to whether various events are good or bad, useful or harmful, worthy of approval or of disapproval, it shares the characteristic of all the social sciences: the lack of absolute predictability common to the natural sciences. *In Preface to Logic*, Morris Raphael Cohen writes: "It is evident that the degree of certainty and the definiteness prevailing in mathematical physics cannot be attained in our knowledge of social phenomena, for the reason that social phenomena are much more complicated, and that the disinterestedness necessary for scientific pursuits is much more difficult of attainment in the social than in the physical realm."[2] This represents the limit of our ability to impose scientific treatment in accounting methodology. Ours is a treatment based on a cognitively rational choice within a social environment. But we believe that, in their particular application to the international petroleum industry, our methods will give more certainty and objectivity to the explanation and description of the local and international environment of the industry. Nevertheless, the problems we face are enormously complex, and we must expect an element of uncertainty and lack of absolute uniqueness in our solutions and selections. Yet, our proposed objective treatment should reduce the degree of uncertainty to manageable levels. It will lessen the problems facing this industry and provide for better informed decision-making.

In order to understand the potential significance of unbiased accounting in dealing with the specific problems of the international petroleum industry, we shall begin our investigation of that industry with a description of perhaps its most controversial problem, i.e. pricing and the distribution of profits.

---

1. Bertrand Russell, "Science and Human Life", *What Is Science?*, James R. Newman, ed., (New York: Washington Square Press, 1961).
2. Morris Raphael Cohen, *Preface to Logic* (New York: Merridian Books, 1956), pp. 172–3.

1.4 The Distribution of Profits

In the Fourth Arab Petroleum Congress held in November 1963 at Beirut, Lebanon, the Organization of Petroleum Exporting Countries (OPEC) concluded that "the governments of OPEC Member Countries in the Middle East are deeply aware of how outmoded the old 50–50 Agreements in the concessions held by the international majors have become".[1]

The Organization of Petroleum Exporting Countries believed that the premises on which the 50–50 agreements were based with respect to pricing no longer existed.[2] For this reason the Organization offered resolutions calling for the restoration of posted prices to their pre-August 1960 level, and for the expensing of royalties in the Middle East. Under the present 50–50 agreements, royalties have little practical significance, for the companies are allowed to deduct them, penny for penny, from their income tax liabilities to the government of the producing country. Thus the distinction between (a) compensation to the owner of the raw material, and (b) taxes to the fiscal authority, has been lost. The companies have attempted to gloss over this distinction. In referring to royalties, a spokesman for one of them said: "What it really boils down to, therefore, is not a question of principle but a matter of hard cash."[3]

These are the attitudes of the petroleum exporting governments and some of the international oil companies as expressed in official pronouncements of their principles. We shall examine the reasoning behind these statements as objectively as possible as a preliminary step toward determining the size of the profits, since any tax or sharing of profits has to start from a determination of net income.

Thus we find that the subject of one of the basic controversies is the profit-sharing formula that takes 50% in taxes, leaving 50% for the company. The pertinent question is, of course, 50% of what? This is where determination of pre-tax net income arises. In such a determination, two basic factors are involved. The first relates to revenues and market prices, while the other relates to costs, especially royalties, and joint costs. However, costs and revenues are sometimes interwoven, as are assets. Accordingly,

---

1. Organization of Petroleum Exporting Countries, *Radical Changes in the International Oil Industry During the Past Decade*, IVth Arab Petroleum Congress, Beirut, November 5–12, 1963, p. 17. (Proceedings are in English.)
2. *Ibid.*, p. 17.
3. *Ibid.*, p. 18.

market prices, royalties, joint costs and reported assets have to be examined objectively before any accurate representation of values can be portrayed.

1.4.A. The Price Controversy

Crude oil and refined products for the international market are priced in a way which is different from the competitive pattern of other commodities.

In the international petroleum market there is a unique system of pricing, generally called the "posted price system". Prices are announced by buyers rather than by sellers. Prices in this situation are administered prices and follow the pattern of price leaders and followers in an oligopolistic market. The complex history of pricing development in this industry is not relevant to our study except with respect to the determination of an arms-length price.[1]

In an international petroleum organization the producing company is little more than a department in a larger organization. The selling and buying occurring between a subsidiary and its parent or parents is only a matter of transfer from a producing department to a sales or marketing department. This price is a paper transfer price, which is sufficient for legal purposes, e.g. transfer of title, evidence of debt but not necessarily in an accounting context. There is no independence in these transactions to assure an unbiased determination of revenues.

A small portion of these organizations' total sales is made to non-affiliated companies at prices normally far below the posted prices, but these sales do not represent a major activity for them. The sales are marginal, based on incremental pricing principles. In the petroleum industry the marginal barrel costs a producer almost nothing to produce, perhaps a few cents for variable expenses. Accordingly, these sales are treated as profitable even though they are made well below the posted prices. This area of competition could have been used as a method of measuring an arm's-length price were it not too small in comparison with total sales to be representative of the sales activities. The most representative sale is one which is, in effect, a transfer of production based upon a non-competitive transfer price.

---

1. Wayne A. Leeman, *The Price of Middle East Oil* (Ithaca, New York: Cornell University Press, 1962). See also: J. E. Hartshorn, *Oil Companies and Governments* (London: Faber & Faber, 1962).

1.4.B. Views of the Organization of Petroleum Exporting Countries

The pricing problem continues to be the most critical factor affecting the relations between international petroleum organizations and the host exporting governments. Crude oil posted prices were reduced in February 1959 and in August 1960, and these reductions were the prime movers for the establishment of the Organization of Petroleum Exporting Countries soon after August 1960. Salient among the underlying reasons for the movement was the practice on the part of oil companies of setting prices unilaterally without consulting with the producing governments. In reaction, the Organization adopted resolution IV.32 in the Fourth Conference:

The Conference, considering

1. That the Member Countries, acting in pursuance of Resolution 1.1, duly protested against the price Reduction affected by the Oil Companies, in August, 1960;
2. That the Oil Companies have so far taken no steps to restore prices to the pre-August, 1960 level;
3. That oil production in all Member Countries is the most prominent source of revenue for financing the implementation of projects of economic development and social progress, and that a fall in crude oil prices reduces the level of oil revenue, thereby bringing about a setback in the realization of the above objectives and seriously dislocating the economy of the Member Countries;
4. That a fall in crude oil prices impairs the purchasing power of Member Countries in respect of manufactured goods which are fundamental to the economy of developing nations and the prices of which have been steadily rising while those of crude oil have been falling;
5. That the oil industry having the character of a public utility, Member Countries cannot be indifferent to such a vital element of the industry as the determination of the price of oil;

RECOMMENDS

That Member Countries should forthwith enter into negoriations with the Oil Companies concerned and/or any authority or body deemed appropriate, with a view to ensuring that oil produced in Member Countries shall be paid for on the basis of posted prices not lower than those which applied prior to August, 1960. If within a reasonable period after the commencement of the negotiations no satisfactory arrangement is reached, the Member Countries shall consult with each other with a view to taking such steps as they deem appropriate in order to restore crude oil prices to the level which prevailed prior to August, 1960; and in any event a report as to the result of negotiations shall be submitted to the Fifth Conference for decision in the light of this paragraph. That Member Countries shall jointly formulate a rational price structure to guide their long-term price policy, on which subject the Board of Governors is hereby directed to prepare a comprehensive study at the earliest possible date. An important element of the price structure to be devised will be the linking of crude oil prices to an index of prices of goods which the Member Countries need to import.[1]

The Organization of Petroleum Exporting Countries also issued explanatory memoranda to substantiate its resolutions, which reported that Persian Gulf posted prices are at their lowest since 1953, that the revenue per barrel has decreased, and that prices of imports to producing countries have increased. They further emphasize the fact that crude oil is a non-renewable resource and that this must be an important factor in royalty determination.

Because the per-barrel revenues have decreased in the production stage, the organization of Petroleum Exporting Countries argued that they necessarily must have increased in subsequent stages. That is, if ultimate prices charged to the final consumer and costs remained constant, the lower prices for crude must produce higher revenues in subsequent stages. The Organization uses these facts to argue that the transfer prices are inadequate measures of revenues. Accurate and unbiased accounting data could be used in such a situation to evaluate prices objectively.

1.4.C. A Petroleum Organization's Views

Representative of the international petroleum industry's views is the Royal Dutch Shell study, "Current International Oil Pricing Problems". The paper deals with a number of pricing problems in a way that might be useful in the determination of revenues. However, as far as the demands of the

---

1. Organization of Petroleum Exporting Countries, "Explanatory Memoranda on the OPEC Resolutions", Geneva, July, 1962.

Organization of Petroleum Exporting Countries are concerned, the paper concludes:

> ... the Governments of the producing countries maintain that oil prices are too low, whereas the Governments of many consuming countries think they are too high. The oil industry operates on a commercial basis, which means that this traditional conflict of interest is reconciled via the pricing mechanism.[1]

> The oil industry is still passing through a period of transition in two respects, both of which contribute to a lack of orderliness in the international oil price situation. In the first place, the industry is still coming to terms with the surplus capacity which has developed since 1957. Owing to a lack of mobility of oil investment from country to country, price discrepancies have developed which will take time to eliminate, although a process of re-adjustment is already operating. In the second place, consuming areas are relying in varying degrees on local refining capacity, which means that locally established prices, and prices related to postings at main export centres, have varying application from one area to another.[2]

Thus the international petroleum industry, for the time being, is not certain what to do about the demands of the Organization of Petroleum Exporting Countries. No definite steps have been taken by either party, although negotiations have been taking place for several years. Nevertheless, the oil industry seems to expect the price mechanism, which is in a transitional period now, to work out a solution satisfactory to all parties concerned.

1.5. Conclusion

It is clear that the conflict of interests could never be wholly solved by a change in accounting methodology alone, for the problem is political as well as financial. But it is equally clear that the common ground upon which any agreement must be based lies in the availability of objective and unbiased reports of the size of the petroleum industry's costs and revenues. An unbiased statement of the net income of international petroleum

---

1. *Petroleum Intelligence Weekly*, "Special Supplement", September 2, 1963, p. 13.
2. *Ibid.*, p. 11.

organizations would serve both the organizations and the petroleum exporting countries in presenting and defending their interests.

Although the interests of the different groups in accounting data are not identical, and may even be conflicting, the purposes for which such data are used have similar characteristics. A tax agency, for example, frequently wishes to enlarge taxable income, while the business organization naturally wishes to decrease it. Yet, accounting methodology must always be utilitarian: it must always serve the goals for which the agency applies it. It will be our goal in this book to demonstrate that, despite the purposes for which accounting methodology is used, only those methods which are more objective actually achieve the goals of accounting. In the international petroleum industry, only those methods which lead to undistorted accounting data are wholly beneficial to all.

CHAPTER II

A Systematic Choice

A DECISION-MAKER faced with a problem to solve can normally exercise his choice as to the course of action (decision) he follows to arrive at a solution by examining the alternatives available to him in the light of a certain established choice criteria. The problem or problems facing him arise in the process of exerting efforts to achieve a certain objective. In other words, the decision-maker having in mind a goal or a set of goals to achieve would investigate the means conducive to the achievement of his objective, choosing those that serve the achievement of such objective best in terms of a certain set of choice criteria. The goal, the set of choice criteria, and the alternatives available for achieving such a goal must be established before any choice (decision) can be exercised among the available courses of action.

2.1. Choice Processes

Either absolute or limited rationality can be assumed in the decision-maker's choice of one alternative against another. Absolute rationality assumes that, "(1) ... all the alternatives of choice are 'given', (2) ... all the consequences attached to each alternative are known ..." and that decision-maker "(3) has a complete utility ordering (or cardinal function) for all possible sets of consequences".[1]

Even with the modifications for risk and uncertainty, it seems to be too demanding on the decision-maker's ability to acquire knowledge of the existing real alternatives, consequences, and utilities. March and Simon state

1. James G. March and Herbert A. Simon, with the collaboration of Harold Guetzkow, *Organizations* (New York: John Wiley, 1958), p. 138.

that, "From a phenomenological viewpoint we can only speak of rationality relative to a frame of reference, and this frame of reference will be determined by the limitations on the rational man's knowledge."[1] In other words, he can only be cognitively rational. His rationality is contained within the amount and quality of information he can accumulate in regard to a given problem within the period in which he must exercise his decision. It is a rational decision at the time it is made and with reference to the set of data used in this process of choice.

This cognitively rational choice and decision-making process represents one of the basic underlying premises of this book.

2.2. *Accounting Principles and Standards*

Periodic income determination represents one of the businessman's problems that require a solution. It is more clearly so in the international oil industry. Between accounting theory and accounting principles, standards, postulates, and techniques, there exist quite a number of alternative ways and means of solution. Some of these principles relate to the basic underlying accounting premises for net income. Others are concerned with recognition and measurement of assets, revenues, costs and other data related directly and indirectly to the income stream. Both categories are generally set in broad terms. Sprouse and Moonitz state that, "The complexities of modern business make it necessary to formulate more specific rules beyond the principles themselves."[2]

To formulate such specific rules in order to help solve the problem of income determination for an oil company as an example, choice has to be exercised among the many rules and techniques (alternatives) that can be delineated and used for arriving at a solution. Should we recognize or ignore the existence of a certain type of asset? Should we measure sales transactions at whatever prices are recorded, or otherwise? Should we use capitalization or expensing techniques in the treatment of exploration costs for income determination purposes? How should assets that are admittedly recognizable be measured? And why? What kind of income and other accounting and business data should be disclosed to the public? And why?

---

1. *Ibid.*
2. Robert T. Sprouse and Maurice Moonitz, *A Tentative Set of Broad Accounting Principles for Business Enterprises* (New York: American Institute of CPAs, 1962), p. 1.

What considerations must be observed in the preparation of managerial reports? And why?

An endless list of questions arises in the process of present day business problem solving; a significant number of such questions relate directly or indirectly to the accounting recognition and measurement techniques of financial events in helping an organization to face problems and solve them.

Questions of this nature and many others can, to a great extent, be delineated in many practical accounting situations. Alternative accounting recognition and measurement techniques of certain other financial events related to the enterprise are not quite as susceptible to a similar delineation. Moreover, a basic and general objective to be fulfilled as a result of the exercise of choice among whatever alternatives are to be considered is also lacking in many situations. It follows that, should such a basic objective be stated clearly, the decision-maker must be provided with a certain set of choice-criteria in order to enable him to make a decision that is at least cognitively rational. It is one of the primary aims of this study to establish such a frame of reference and goal-oriented choice criteria in an accounting context. At least it is proposed as an attempt in the right direction as far as income determination in the international petroleum industry is concerned.

In other words, this study will establish the set of specific rules for accounting recognition and all measurement of financial events in the industry referred to above. The pool of alternatives to be used for exercising the choice of those most conducive to an established objective is not necessarily limited to the recognition and measurement techniques available in the accounting literature or practiced by accountants.

Striving for rationality, we shall draw on alternatives available in other fields of knowledge that are concerned with similar phenomena, such as economics and mathematics. This is believed to be conducive to a better choice of applicable techniques, through a consideration of an enlarged list of alternatives.

In order to be able to investigate such specific rules and techniques (alternatives), an examination of the basic underlying general premises is necessarily called for. These are the foundations on which techniques are built. An examination of a structure without testing its foundation is, no doubt, incomplete. We are attempting to present as complete a picture for income determination in the industry concerned as is possible within the present state of our limited knowledge. Hence the work hereafter presented is closely connected with the problems of assets, revenues, and cost recognition and measurement, to the exclusion of other problems not so closely related to our basic objective. Only a reference to them will be made in the final chapter. Problems of accounting disclosure and reporting will be touched upon only lightly in the process of delineating the income determination question. It is necessary to do so in order to indicate their relative irrelevance to the basic theme of the study.

2.3. Theory of the Neutral Value of Net Income

The outcome of this research is presented in Chapter XII in the form of a theoretical structure, called "accounting theory of the neutral value of net income". The crux of the theory is twofold. First, it differentiates between purely abstract and generally basic premises of accounting income theory and those premises that are of an empirical particular nature. In this manner it is contained in two basic divisions, one abstract and one particular, the latter oriented toward the international petroleum industry.

Application of the above-mentioned theory is made in Chapter XIII, utilizing data available in an annual study published by the Chase Manhattan Bank called "Petroleum Industry 19...".[1] The utilization requires certain approximations which are explained throughout the text or the chapter.

2.4. Toward Establishing Goal-Oriented Choice Criteria

We have indicated in section 2.2 that specific alternative recognition and measurement techniques should be delineated, that a general underlying goal should be established, and that choice criteria should be somehow related to the goal and the alternative means directed to its achievement.

This seemingly is in line with the theory of rational choice, introduced by March and Simon, which "incorporates two fundamental characteristics: (1) Choice is always exercised with respect to a limited, approximate, simplified 'model' of the real situation ...",[2] which they refer to as the chooser's "definition of the situation".[3] The other characteristic the authors emphasize is that "(2) The elements of the definition of the situation are not 'given'

---

1. The Chase Manhattan Bank, *Annual Analysis of the Petroleum Industry* (September 1961).
2. March and Simon, *op. cit.,* p. 139.
3. The Chase Manhattan Bank, *op. cit.*

...".[1] explaining that they are not taken as constituent data of the theory of rational choice. They further add that such elements are "themselves the outcome of psychological and sociological processes, including the chooser's own activities and the activities of others in his environment".[2]

Our problem, we should like to emphasize, is to determine income, that is, to choose a set of recognition and measurement techniques the outcome of whose application would be the determination of such income. Nevertheless, before exercising our choice, we should have a "model of real situation", a simplified one to be sure. In other words, we should define the situation in which an international oil company exists. This is the first requirement of the theory of rational choice, as was stated above. The elements of the definition of such a situation are to be derived as a result of the activities of the oil company concerned and others existing in its internal environment. This is the second requirement of the theory.

Accordingly, a simplified model of the real situation must be constructed. This is the subject of the following chapter, which explains in abstract terms the systematic operating mechanisms of business organizations, emphasizing the significance of accounting data for its decision-making processes. It is a homeostatic organization model, the goal of which is security and survival. It is a biological analogy in a business environment.

The factors that supposedly affect the survival of an international oil company are considered as part of the organization's own activities and those of others existing in its environment. For convenience and clarification, the factors belonging to the organization's own activities are referred to as factors belonging to its internal environment. Those derived from the activities of others are referred to as factors belonging to its external environment. Whenever reference is made to both categories together, the term "environmental variables" is used. The elements of the model are thus reconstructed to take into consideration environmental variables, as long as such variables affect, or are affected by, the choice of accounting recognition and measurement techniques. This is done in Chapter IV. Hence the circle is completed; the model is built with elements based on environmental activities. An important portion of the theory of rational choice is applied.

---

1. *Ibid.*
2. *Ibid.*

2.5. The General Choice Criteria

Given a number of alternatives to choose from and a goal-oriented model of the real situation with elements derived from its environment, compatibility with this basic goal is one the basic considerations in any choice process, be it of broad business alternatives or narrowly defined techniques. In other words, the set of recognition and measurement techniques that produces a periodic income quantification that is most contributive to the survival of the organization, within a certain definition of the situation, is the one to be chosen.

As a result of the conflicting pressures and interests in the periodic net income of an international oil company, it is concluded that the least biased quantification of such income would be most contributive to the enterprise survival. This leads us to the second element of our choice criteria. As far as an oil company belonging to the international petroleum industry is concerned, a biased determination of net income would be unfavorable to its survival, whereas an unbiased one would be otherwise. Hence, only those recognition and measurement techniques that strive for an unbiased determination of net income should be chosen, so that the organization's basic goal is served properly.

2.6. The Basic Accounting Frame of Reference

To determine which accounting premises and techniques strive most for an unbiased determination of net income requires a certain set of characteristics to serve as a guide line in the delineation, examination, and evaluation of recognition and measurement alternatives, as a first step toward exercising a rational choice. The following propositions are offered as basic characteristics underlying the choice of recognition and measurement techniques for qualifying as determinants of an unbiased net income for a petroleum-producing organization belonging to the international petroleum industry.

2.6.A. An Historical Cost Basis

Cost is defined by Sprouse and Moonitz as "a forgoing, a sacrifice made to secure benefits and is measured by an exchange price".[1] At any point in time, resources and benefits belonging to the organization (to the entity)

---

1. *Ibid.*

could have been acquired through an exchange transaction or through other means such as the discovery of an oil field. Whenever an exchange price for such assets and benefits exists, it is used as the basis of the original recording and all subsequent allocations, reallocations, and recordings so long as such benefits are still in the possession of the said organization. Should such an acquisition exchange price or a market place for such acquired assets or benefits be nonexistent, an equivalent fair value of the said resources is taken to be the basis of the original and subsequent recordings. This is considered as an acceptable, objectively determined substitute for an acquisition price. Both exchange prices (costs) underlie our chosen measurement techniques for the determination of net income from hydrocarbon production operations for a business organization belonging to the international oil industry. It is an historical cost basis.

2.6. B. Cost Allocation: a Reflection of Physical Regrouping

Taking an historical cost basis as our starting point, we find that problems of cost allocation arise, particularly in accounting for manufacturing, process and extractive industries. It is generally true that, in the production, processing, or manufacturing operations, the factors of production are regrouped to the extent that the outgoing commodity is an outcome of such regrouping, be it materials, machines, or otherwise. Such physical regrouping, to be accomplished, must be accompanied by managerial and human efforts. Without a monetary reflection of this historical state of affairs, no recording and subsequent determination of product or process cost can be achieved. Hence, original historical costs must be regrouped, in a manner that reflects such historical physical and human effort regrouping.

In other word, such regrouped (allocated) costs attach to whatever regrouping of physical substances and human efforts have been expended to produce, extract, or make available a product in its outgoing form. These are the specific new groups of costs, which are described by Paton and Littleton to "possess real significance".[1]

Hence market value connotations and other similar criteria are ruled out as primary bases for cost allocation, by virtue of the historical cost and the physical regrouping propositions. The latter represents our basic choice criteria for common and joint cost allocation.

---

1. W. A. Paton and A. C. Littleton, *An Introduction to Corporate Accounting Standards* (Columbus, Ohio: American Accounting Association, 1957) p. lx.

2.6.C. *Accounting for a Profit-oriented Organization*

It is not necessary to assume that the basic objective of the conceptual organization under consideration is to earn profit. Making a positive profit is taken to be one of the critical factors affecting the viability, continuity, and survival of the said organization. It is one of the essential elements of the model and an integral part of our simplified definition of the real situation.

It is narrowed down, however, to the hydrocarbon production stage of a business organization belonging to the international petroleum industry. This procedure is followed because of the fact that most of the significant accounting questions arise in this stage as do most of the environmental variables. This is not to minimize the importance of subsequent stages, nor is it intended to reflect any lack of significance concerning the organizational, managerial, or accounting questions that relate to such downstream operations.

2.6.D. *Arm's-length Prices or Their Equivalent*

The conventional accounting discipline arrives at asset, cost, revenue, and expense data through the utilization of initial exchange prices and subsequent allocations and regroupings of said prices. F. Sewell bray states that "the primary basis of accounting lies in records of exchange dealings or their equivalents, conveniently classified within group definitions, at present largely promulgated to conform with entity needs".[1] His views are in conformity with the conventional recording and grouping basis.

Needless to say, the exchange prices or their equivalent, to be meaningful, must be an outcome of arm's-length transactions, i.e. transactions between parties that have complete verifiable independence in their decision to consummate a certain transaction at a certain price. Maurice Moonitz defines an exchange price to be "the consideration given or the 'sacrifice' made in an exchange".[2] He further adds that this price is "the proper basis for purposes of initial recording",[3] indicating that for this price to be applicable to specific cases, the condition that "arm's length bargaining between two

---

1. F. Sewell Bray, *The Accounting Mission* (Melbourne: Melbourne University Press, 1951), p. 27.
2. Maurice Moonitz, *The Basic Postulates of Accounting* (New York: American Institute of CPAs, 1961), p. 29.
3. *Ibid.*

(or more) independent entities, or evidence that is the equivalence of this standard"[1] must be met.

Hence, prices based on arm's-length transactions or their equivalents are still another choice criterion to be observed throughout the process of choosing the determinants of net income. This is particularly so in the determination of hydrocarbon production revenues to be examined in Chapter VII.

2.6.E. *Neutral, Unbiased and Objective*

We have seen, in section 2.4, that a basic condition for exercising rational choice is the existence of at least a simplified model of the real situation; it is the chooser's definition of the situation. It was also stated previously that limitations on the chooser's knowledge attribute relativity to his rationality to the extent that his rationality becomes only cognitive rather than absolute. In other words, at least a realistic though rather simplified reflection of existing situations is called for. Hence the practical phenomena which we are examining, and which have a bearing on our income determination must be transformed to accounting data that reflect a realistic, though probably simplified, picture of the happenings and occurrences attributable to the said practical phenomena. The accounting transformation process takes the form of recognizing such happenings and occurrences and providing for measuring them in a manner serviceable to the organization's goal or sub-goals. This reflection transformation process is part of the model; it is part of the elements of the situation and its definition. And, since we are required to have a realistic model of the situation, it follows that any portion thereof must also be realistic.

We are reminded, however that there are limits on the information and knowledge we can obtain. The real world is highly complex. The picture we draw for it, with such limits to our knowledge, must necessarily be simplified; in fact, it might even be highly approximate. Nevertheless, it is an operational and logical necessity to draw one that, to the best of our knowledge, is representative of existing situations. Our picture, in a way, is not an exact replica of the original. The best we can do is to improve the picture we draw as our knowledge about our model increases. In some cases, and within our framework, we might be able to measure "exactly" an initial exchange price. Subsequent regrouped measurements do not possess

---

1. *Ibid.*

the same degree of exactness because of our incomplete knowledge in identifying the regrouped initial costs or exchange prices with the regrouped physical picture. This underlies the "limit-value measurement" concept to be introduced in Chapter V. It also underlies the whole schematic approach to the problems of accounting recognition and measurement throughout this study. Since we are lacking in our ability to establish exact, factual, and absolutely objective measurements, our frame of reference allows us to be satisfied with answers consistent with said frame of reference.

It is only within this limited sense of relatively realistic models of existing situations that certain recognition and measurement techniques are neutral, unbiased and comparatively more objective than others. Neutrality and objectivity as used in this study are not absolute: rather they are relative to certain defined points of departure.

2.6. F. *Flexibility and Operationality*

Without violating the spirit of the frame of reference introduced above, flexibility and operationality are two desirable characteristics of the tools to be utilized, be they analytical or related to recognition and measurement problems. They are desirable because they facilitate handling practical empirical phenomena within given limited budgets of time and resources. Flexibility of a certain tool is defined as its relative ability to handle certain defined problems faster and clearer than others, whereas operationality is the characteristic of facing the problem within an empirical practical context rather than a relatively abstract one.

2.7. *The Process of Choosing by Elimination*

Choice criteria, together with the basic organizational and accounting frame of reference, have already been covered. The model with elements related to income determination based on activities taking place in the internal and external environment of a business organization belonging to the international petroleum industry has already been referred to as the subject of Chapters III and IV, with the outcome of the study being introduced in Chapter XII as the theory of the neutral value of net income, with a semi-empirical illustration in Chapter XIII. In Chapter V, the model is examined in its relationship with the basic conventional accounting premises as a preliminary step toward the investigation and selection of recognition and measurement techniques to take place in Chapters VI through XII.

A representative portrayal of the present system of revenue and cost determination in the international petroleum industry is presented in Chapter VI, explicitly oriented toward the hydrocarbon production stage.

Chapter VII examines the alternative techniques of determining revenues as a step toward the selection of the one that is consistent with the accounting frame of reference presented in section 2.6 above.

The problem of joint costs in the production of hydrocarbons with questions of allocation, expensing, and capitalization are the subject of Chapters VIII through X. This is part of examining the alternatives of cost and expense determination and choosing those that satisfy the choice criteria introduced above.

The question of royalties and determining the cost of goods sold and that of inventories being affected by the method used in joint cost allocation is examined immediately after concluding the introduction of a joint cost allocation method consistent with the above-mentioned choice criteria. Hence it is the subject of Chapter XI. Between Chapters V and XI the process of delineating available income determination alternatives, investigating them, and choosing the relatively unbiased ones is completed. All this is done in light of the basic accounting premises, the accounting frame of reference, and the organization model, which are the subjects of Chapters II through IV. During the process of delineating alternatives and exercising a choice among them, they are consistently eliminated until only one remains which is more satisfactory than the others within a defined situation. Should a superior alternative appear later, it should replace the previously chosen one. Similarly, if the basic frame of reference is modified, added to, or subtracted from, the process of choice must be repeated and other alternatives given a new chance of winning.

Thus the mission is accomplished and the goal is achieved. However, research in this area of organization and accounting theory does not seem to have an end. Other related research problems and feasible extensions of the work presented in the study are the subject of the final chapter, Chapter XIV.

2.8. The Conclusion

Accounting theory of the neutral value of net income introduced in this study is the outcome of applying objective methodology to the conventional income determination concepts and formulae. In form it is not drastically different from the conventional theory; the essential difference lies in its substance, in the approach and methodology it uses, and in its underlying necessary conditions and premises.

In this book, the theory is adapted to the international petroleum industry because of the challenges that this industry introduces to the conventional accounting theory and techniques. Such challenges cannot be satisfied through the conventional accounting concepts and practices alone, but must be supplemented by newly developed techniques. For this purpose we have developed the accounting theory of the neutral value of net income. It draws from the pool of conventional accounting concepts those techniques which are consistent and objective in determining the value of income. Where we have found the conventional theory deficient we have substituted wholly new techniques. The theory of the neutral value of net income contributes to accounting concepts by providing incremental extensions to recognition and measurement of assets, revenues, and expenses. This is done with one basic objective in mind: that the theory developed should be unbiased, impartial, and neutral, devoid of human personal preferences except insofar as it serves the organization's basic goal, and, finally, consistent and objective rather than contradictory and subjective.

CHAPTER III

Accounting Data:
An Information-Communication Problem
in an Organizational Model

WE HAVE seen in the previous chapter that, in order to achieve our objective of evaluating the applications of accounting theory in a certain industry, we should have a conceptual representation of at least one entity in that industry. This is particularly true if a case study of any one real entity is neither practically feasible nor analytically useful for our objective. Hence, in the international petroleum industry, organizational relationships between parents and subsidiaries are extremely complex, to the extent that such relationships themselves require an operational tool capable of explaining practical phenomena reflecting the interactions of such relationships. A case study would, in this instance, necessarily restrict our examination to a particular entity, thus depriving us of utilizing evidence and data available for the much wider and richer spectrum of the international petroleum industry. This is in addition to the fact that access to data and evidence in any one single international oil company is next to impossible, since the expression of such views and the publication of the real organizational behavior within any one company might have some harmful effects on its competitive position and on its relations with those that may have an influence on the outcome of its operations.

Hence the conceptual representation of any international oil company, and not any particular one, is made in the form of an organizational model to be explained and elaborated in this chapter. However, since the model is not constructed in a vacuum and is necessarily built to serve as an operational tool for our accounting evaluation purposes, the position of accounting data in relation to this proposed model must be clarified. In other words, the relationship between accounting and organization theory has to be established in a more systematic manner. The usefulness of accounting data and the effect of accounting practices upon organizational behavior and decisions have also to be established in order to justify the utilization of such a model as an operational tool for evaluation of accounting as applied in the international petroleum industry.

Such clarification and establishment of justification premises is built into the construction of the model itself and into the application of the model to the international oil industry. This will take place in Chapter IV.

Furthermore, a number of methodological alternative approaches to the construction of this model are examined as a first step in choosing the one alternative that is most useful for our purposes.

3.1. *Organizations and Accounting*

It is agreed that accounting is utilitarian. Its *raison d'être* is to serve the purposes of the different groups interested in financial and cost data related to the business organization. Such data affect and are affected by the nature of the organization and its behavior. All parts of an organization are in need of objective accounting data for the satisfaction of their individual purposes and common goals. Yet we must recognize that each part of the organization serves also as an element of the environment of the organization. It might be more convenient, then, to refer to accounting as a system that serves the environment of the organization; that is; it serves the objectives of the constituents of the environment. Perhaps we should refer to accounting as a subsystem of the organization serving its environment. The whole setup might be referred to as a system and every individual tool as a subsystem. Be that as it may, a rational choice has to be made among the several alternative approaches to the conceptual representation of such a system. All the enumerated alternatives that follow strive in one way or another for this conceptual representation of a business entity. They achieve such an objective in varying degrees of clarity and realism as to the reflection of a relatively more complete and more accurate picture of a practical situation. They differ also in their degree of flexibility and capability to cope with constantly changing practical and environmental conditions of such business organizations. In other words, they differ in their inherent characteristics as to the degree of clarity and realism in explaining the practical phenomena of such organizations with which we are concerned. The alternative that possesses more clarity and realism than others in its reflection of practical situations, particularly for our purposes stated above, is the one we shall choose as an operational tool for application throughout the rest of this study. It is the alternative which is also characterized as being more flexible than others in coping with constantly changing practical conditions in the industry with which we are concerned.

3.1. A. Economic Theory of the Firm: Does It Serve the Purpose?

For many years social scientists have been attempting to simulate the natural sciences in their analytical approach. Economists have elaborated in their models an abstract yet factual picture of the economy and its constituents. Many macro- and micro-economic theories have been developed over the years. Nevertheless, economic theorists are often too limited in the choice of their variables. Most commonly they have no room for man with all his shortcomings; yet, because man is obviously essential to the nature of organizations, we must include the requisite variables in the theory in order to draw a more realistic structure.

In other words, the economic theory of the firm, though useful in economic analysis, does not possess sufficient realism in its reflection of practical phenomena involving men who are only cognitively and not absolutely rational. Furthermore, the above-mentioned theory is not flexible enough as far as its capability to cope with the problems we face in the international petroleum industry. This is so because of the limited number of variables that it takes into consideration in comparison with variables that have to be considered in an accounting examination of the industry, as will be explained in Chapter IV.

This, though, is merely a reference to one of the alternatives available to us as a frame of reference for our approach to income determination in the international petroleum industry. It is a sufficient condition for considering the economic theory of the firm not useful enough for our purposes. Hence this is not intended to be a critique of the theory of the firm, since literature on organization and economics is rich in this respect, and any attempt here would be repetitive.

Starting from the economic theory of the firm, "administration architects" began to build a different structure, which started with observed phenomena and led to courses of action. The structure they build was similar to aerial photographs of land, which are exact copies of the land's surface displayed in a manageable size and used, perhaps, as a basis for choosing the routing of a new highway. There are many routes, but from an ideal vantage point it can be seen that only one is relatively more satisfactory in serving the objective underlying the decision to build a road. Structures different from those offered by the economists have been developed because the inductive method of the "administration architects" was diametrically opposed to the deductive logic of the micro-economic theorists.

3.1.B. The Definition of an Organization

To the layman the word "organization" might convey some sort of systemization and arrangement. It does not normally convey the picture of a complete integrated system; rather it is a function of, or an action of, systemization. In fact, even in the literature on business management we find that many textbook writers use the term "organization" to mean merely one of the fundamental functions of management. For example, one of the standard definitions of organization is "the arrangement of functions deemed necessary for attainment of the objective and is an indication of the authority and responsibility assigned to individuals charged with the execution of the respective functions".[1] In this definition the meaning of the term is limited almost exclusively to its managerial sense.

However, neither of these meanings is sufficient for our purposes. The crux of our distinction lies in its aggregativeness and unity; it lies in the concept of a system. Its basic characteristic is the co-ordination of the individual efforts for the achievement of a set of goals.[2] The definition given by March and Simon is much more nearly adequate for our purposes: "Organizations are assemblages of interacting human beings and they are the largest assemblages in our society that have anything resembling a central co-ordinative system."[3] This, as the authors explain, is a biological analogy, similar to, though not as highly developed as, the central nervous system in higher biological organisms. The definition I shall adopt for the purpose of this thesis is based on the March and Simon concept, and it differs from their definition only in that it underscores the biological

---

1. George R. Terry, *Principles of Management* (Homewood, Ill.: Richard D. Irwin, 1956), pp. 239–40.
2. Frederick Harbinson and Charles Myers, *Management in the Industrial World* (*An International Analysis*) (New York: McGraw-Hill Book Co., 1959), p. 3.
3. March and Simon, *op. cit.*, p. 4.

analogy. An organization, then, is a complex organic structure of interdependent and subordinate elements whose relations and properties are largely determined by their function in the whole; each element is designated to perform a specific function, and, through the summation of such functions, the whole is constructed to achieve a specific end, which may be, finally, the continuation of the structure; that is, survival. This definition is adopted because of its special relevance to the organization model to be developed in this chapter and because of its usefulness to both the abstract theory and practical experience of business organizations, particularly those belonging to the international petroleum industry.

3.1.C. Choosing the Model

Reviewing the literature on the theory of organization, we find several alternative forms of the organization model. This set of models is representative of the various theoretical structures of formal organization. The difference between them lies in the behavior characteristics of each. They are:

1. The mechanical model, which assumes that the participants in formal organizations are passive instruments. That is, in a generic sense, they resemble machines in the acceptances of instructions and in executing them. This resemblance is emphasized by assuming also that those participants are not capable of initiating action or exerting influence in any significant way.

2. The motivational model, which assumes that the participants in organizations bring with them attitudes, values, and goals. It further assumes that organization members should be motivated in order to participate in the activities of the organization because of the presumption that there is incomplete parallelism between their personal goals and the goals of the organization.

3. The rationality model, which takes into consideration the cognitive limits on rationality, considering participants in organizations as decision-making and problem-solving entities.

This is the first set of alternatives available to us in our choice of a model of organization. Since this thesis is not basically directed toward the evaluation of contemporary organization theory, no extensive critical analysis of these models will be offered. However, one characteristic common to all of them should be mentioned, since this will assist us in developing our choice of a model: no evidence is offered to support the truth of the propositions found in the three models. In fact, it would seem impossible to have evidence for all the propositions, since many are mutually contradictory. Of course, one can say that, if each proposition is consistent with the assumptions on which it is built, there should be no objection. However, if this is correct analytically, little room is left for the original classification. We should prefer an integrated analytical structure; one which integrates the different parts of the theory of organization into one unified, logical structure. To construct such an integrated and general analytical structure is quite beyond the scope of this study.

3.1.D. The Question of Methodology

In choosing our method of approach, we might ask whether there are other methods of conceptual model construction which are more conductive to our purposes than the one proposed by March and Simon. To make such a judgment, we need to compare their approach with other methodological alternatives to determine their relative usefulness in leading to a better understanding of the issues involved in developing an organization model. There are at least four principal methodological alternatives available to us besides the one proposed by March and Simon. They are:

(1) The statistical method

This is essentially the collection of data about organizational problems such as employee turnover, the degree of centralization, and similar information, in a large sample of actual existing organizations. From this collection of statistical data, a cross-section analysis is made in order to obtain certain conclusions about the behavior of the major variables in these organizations. But here we are dealing with empirical phenomena so costly and extensive to collect that it might be non-operational. However, it is superior to the March and Simon method, even if it is only partially utilized as, perhaps, an element of another model.

(2) The modified deductive method

This method involves the grouping of organizational issues under a few titles – coordination, communication, decision-making, for example – and the formulating of a set of principles that are consistent with practical evidence as guides to managerial action in each of these different fields of organization theory. This is in essence the same method used by March and Simon. I find that it lacks the integration and consistency so necessary in the construction of a more realistic framework.

(3) The mathematical construct method

The third method is the building of rigorous mathematical models of organization. This method has been used in many fields of science. However, its usefulness in the social sciences is necessarily limited because of the uncertainty involved in the measurement and definition of the variables and parameters.

So far, none of these alternative approaches to the development of the required model has proved to be useful for our purposes. Such alternatives are either contradictory and lacking in evidence or too costly and laborious to construct without possessing the necessary characteristics of flexibility and a more complete and realistic reflection of practical phenomena. Such being the case, we shall develop the required model, drawing from the work William Ross Ashby[1] for the basic notions of the model. Some of these notions will be elaborated on, especially those related to communication, information regulation, and control. Such elaboration will be in line with the work of Claude E. Shannon and Warren Weaver[2] on one side and Ashby[3] and Weiner[4] on the other. All these borrowed concepts and notions will be integrated into an organization model that reflects business phenomena. It is the homeostatic organization model.

3.2 The Homeostatic Organization Model

Homeostatic is defined as "regulatory".[5] According to this line of

---

1. William Ross Ashby, *An Introduction to Cybernetics* (New York: John Wiley, 1957).
2. Claude E. Shannon and Warren Weaver, *The Mathematical Theory of Communication* (Urbana, Ill.: University of Illinois Press, 1949).
3. Ashby, *op. cit.*.
4. Norbert Weiner, *The Human Use of Human Beings, Cybernetics and Society* (Boston: Houghton Mifflin, 1954).
5. *Ibid.*, p. 196.

development, an organization model begins with the idea of "homeostasis"; that is, of a mechanism for stabilizing a variable or a group of variables within certain limits of toleration.[1]

3.2. *A. Assumptions and Definitions*

A.1. Feedback mechanisms. An organization consists of an aggregate of "governing mechanisms", called control or feedback mechanisms, whose function is to reduce the variable if it rises above the upper limit, or to raise the variable if it falls below the lower limits.

A.2. The goal. In this abstract model the goal of the organization is "survival". As a dynamic system, the organization can be in various states which may occur during its attempt to avoid or to overcome disturbances. Such disturbances are divided into two categories; those which, unalleviated, will lead to the discontinuity of the organization; and those which will not affect its survival even if never assuaged. For illustration, let us suppose that M refers to the different states in which the organization survives where certain essential variables are kept within assigned limits due to the effect of disturbances arising from the organization's environment. Similarly, let non-M refer to the different states in which the organization does not survive and where such essential variables are not kept within their assigned limits due to a different effect of disturbances.

A.3. The essential variables. Let E represent the set of essential variables which affect the survival of the organization, such as the profit rate, the morale of the employees, the share of the market, the minimum level of supplies: let us assume that the organization faces a disturbance, D, which might be internal or external. However, in the organization there is a decision-making unit, R, that is supposed to protect E from D as shown in Fig.3.1.

$$D \longrightarrow R \longrightarrow E$$

Fig. 3.1

A.4. The regulator. R functions as a regulator whose major work is to block the transmission of disturbances, D, to the essential variables, E. D is not meant to refer to disturbances as essential variables E, but rather the

---

1. *Ibid.*

set of disturbances, $\mathcal{D}$, functions as the cause of variations within $\mathcal{E}$. The blocking may take place in different ways, although normally it is the case that the major defense is skilled counteraction. It takes the form of the collection of information about the disturbance, the preparation for its arrival, and, finally, the confrontation of the disturbance. The significance of $\mathcal{R}$ is manifest, for the unmitigated effect of $\mathcal{D}$ on $\mathcal{E}$ is assumed to be critical, and survival is always at stake.

A.5. Regulation. The process of regulation can be considered one of the mitigation of the effects of critical disturbance $\mathcal{D}$ on the essential variables $\mathcal{E}$. The outcome of the interaction between the disturbance $\mathcal{D}$ and the assuaging power of the regulator $\mathcal{R}$ determines the value of $\mathcal{E}$. From all the values of $\mathcal{E}$ only some are compatible with the survival of the organization. Hence the regulator, $\mathcal{R}$, to be successful, must act in a way so related to $\mathcal{D}$ that the outcome is, if possible, always within the acceptable state $\mathcal{M}$.

Let us assume that, at a certain point in time, we start with a given table, T, that gives the outcome of the game between $\mathcal{R}$ and $\mathcal{D}$. If $\mathcal{D}$ takes an arbitrary value, $\mathcal{R}$ takes some value determined by the value of $\mathcal{D}$, and the value that $\mathcal{E}$ will take is given by T which indicates the outcome being either $\mathcal{M}$ or non-$\mathcal{M}$. If $\mathcal{D}$ takes another value, then the process is repeated and so on.

If $\mathcal{R}$ is a very skilful regulator, then it should be able to so mitigate $\mathcal{D}$ that all the outcomes fall within $\mathcal{M}$. In this case, T acts as a sub-set of the decision-making unit $\mathcal{R}$, always so protecting $\mathcal{E}$ from $\mathcal{D}$, so that $\mathcal{E}$ never varies from a survival range within $\mathcal{M}$. This is shown diagrammatically as follows:

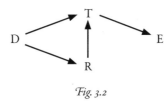

Fig. 3.2

A.6. Communication. "Communication in its broadest sense includes knowledge of the real world; its expression in language and signs; its communicability; its use within social and ethical systems." Such is the definition given by Colin Cherry[1] whereas Warren Weaver includes in communication "all procedures by which one mind may affect another", involving as such "written and oral speech ..." and "all human behavior".[2]

Accordingly, communication in this model is referred to in this broad sense. For illustration let us look back at Fig. 3.2, where the arrows represent channels of communication, and the disturbances, D, follow these lines of communication toward E. Normally, D follows a path through R and T to E. If R does not change its value or does not communicate its change, D passes directly through T. Depending on the blocking power of T and the disturbing influence of D, E may or may not be maintained at a survival level.

Let us consider R as a transmitter and discuss this portion of Fig. 3.2:

$$D \longrightarrow R \longrightarrow T$$

Accordingly to the Law of Requisite Variety, R's capacity as a regulator cannot exceed R's capacity as a channel of communication. This is what Shannon gives in theorem 10, which says that if noise appears in a message, the amount of noise of disturbance that can be removed by a correction channel, i.e. regulator R, is limited to the amount of information that can be carried by the channel.[3]

A.7. Control. Let us now introduce another variable to our system. Suppose that the decisions made by R must represent the wishes of a controlling body such as a Board of Directors C. This is expressed diagrammatically as follows:

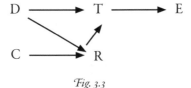

Fig. 3.3

1. A. J. Ayer *et al.*, *Studies in Communication*, contributions by A. J. Ayer, J. B. S. Haldane, Colin Cherry, Sir Geoffrey Vickers, J. Z. Young, R. Wittkower, T. B. L. Webster, Randolph Quirk and D. B. Fry with an introduction by B. Ifor Evans (London: Secker & Warburg, 1955).; see Colin Cherry, *Communication Theory and Human Behavior*, p. 45; see also A. J. Ayer, *What Is Communication?*, p. 11.
2. Shannon and Weaver, *op. cit.* p. 95.
3. *Ibid.*, p. 37.

If $\mathcal{R}$ is a perfect regulator, $\mathcal{C}$ can have complete control over the outcome in spite of the entrance of disturbances by way of $\mathcal{D}$. Thus, if an attempt at control is made by $\mathcal{C}$ or $\mathcal{E}$, then,

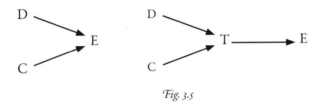

$$C \longrightarrow E$$

Fig. 3.4

is disturbed by $\mathcal{D}$ so that the connection is:

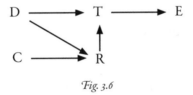

Fig. 3.5

then a regulator $\mathcal{R}$, taking information from both $\mathcal{C}$ and $\mathcal{D}$ and located between $\mathcal{C}$ and T,

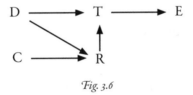

Fig. 3.6

may be able to form with T a compound channel to $\mathcal{E}$ that transmits fully from $\mathcal{C}$ while transmitting nothing from $\mathcal{D}$. Accordingly, the achievement of control depends as essentially on the achievement of regulation as it does on the effectiveness of communication.

3.2. B. Modification of the Model

B.1. Variant assumptions

(a) $\mathcal{D}$ may be a vector representing many compound disturbances with any number of components.

(b) The target also may be a compound one. It may happen that the acceptable states, $\mathcal{M}$, may be a vector with more than one component and that it may be defined in the form of separate specifications for each component.

(c) Internal complexities might also be introduced to the model. Suppose that the major problem is the interaction between several regulations. There is nothing in the previous formulation that prevents the quantities or states or elements in $\mathcal{D}$, $\mathcal{R}$, $\mathcal{T}$, or $\mathcal{E}$ from being made of interrelated parts.

B.2. The imperfect regulator. Suppose that perfect regulation is not possible and we wish the regulation to be as good as is possible in the given conditions. For example, suppose that $\mathcal{R}$'s capacity as a channel for transmitting information from $\mathcal{D}$ to $\mathcal{T}$ becomes insufficient to maintain the limit of variables in $\mathcal{E}$ at a survival level. When this occurs, the regulation is necessarily imperfect.

To overcome such difficulties, $\mathcal{R}$ may perform its work before $\mathcal{T}$ starts to move and to forestall the disaster. However, there are many important cases in which anticipation is impossible. This happens when $\mathcal{R}$'s action cannot be completed before the outcome, at $\mathcal{T}$, starts to be determined. The solution in such cases is to increase the speed of transmission of the information from $\mathcal{D}$ to $\mathcal{R}$. Sometimes, however, the resources of the organization do not permit such a speeding up of the transmission through $\mathcal{R}$ and $\mathcal{R}$'s reactions cannot be transmitted to $\mathcal{T}$ before the outcome takes place. All that can be done in these cases is to make the imperfect regulator as good as possible under the given circumstances.

In some cases the regulator cannot be informed about the disturbances before $\mathcal{E}$ is affected. In these cases the information from $\mathcal{D}$ to $\mathcal{R}$ comes through $\mathcal{T}$. Thus, instead of:

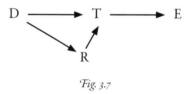

Fig. 3.7

we have:

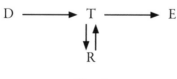

Fig. 3.8

In other cases the information may be forced to take a longer route before it gets to $\mathcal{R}$. It might not be informed until $\mathcal{E}$ has already been affected, as shown in Fig. 3.9:

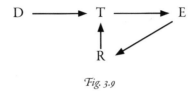

Fig. 3.9

B.3. Continuity and Errors. We have assumed that the states of the survival of the organization were divided into $\mathcal{M}$ and non-$\mathcal{M}$ and that non-$\mathcal{M}$ was completely incompatible with regulation. However, it might happen that some systems show continuity, so that the values of the essential variables lie along a scale of undesirability. The presence of continuity makes possible a regulation of great practical importance in spite of its imperfection. In these favorable circumstances small errors are allowed to occur, transmitting information to $\mathcal{R}$ so that greater errors may be avoided. In terms of communication, this is the concept of the simple feedback regulator.

3.3. The Relationship between the Homeostatic Model and the Other Models of Organization

The core of the model is the decision-making process which considers an organization as an information-processing system. It collects certain information about the organizational problems, studies it, and issues certain instructions to the governing mechanisms. This may be applied in a practical situation to describe organizational behavior. However, there is a missing link in the chain, and it relates to the basis on which the information is studied and to the criteria on which the instructions to the governing mechanisms are based. It is at this point that the cognitive model of March and Simon[1] can be connected to the model.

Here we obtain the criteria of satisfying rather than maximizing which is consistent with the upper and lower limits of the values of the variables in the homeostatic model.

Another large field of inquiry in the subject arises when $\mathcal{D}$ and $\mathcal{R}$ in the homeostatic model are vectors and when the compound that leads eventually to the outcome in $\mathcal{T}$ or $\mathcal{E}$ is so distributed in time that the components of

---

1. A. J. Ayer *et al.*, *Ibid.*

$\mathcal{D}$ and $\mathcal{R}$ occur alternately. Here we have the whole disturbance presented and the whole response evoked, each consisting of a sequence of sub-disturbances and sub-responses. The outcome in such a case will depend on some relationship between the whole disturbance presented and the whole response evoked. Yet this is more properly related to game theory in mathematics than to economics. Indeed, in mathematics this is the Theory of Games and Strategies founded by von Neumann. However, this area does allow vast possibilities for integrating the theory of games into the theory of organization.

If we leave the decision-making unit and move to the governing mechanisms themselves, we find that the homeostatic model generally assumes the obedience of these mechanisms to the instructions issued to them. In this, it resembles the mechanical model of March and Simon in considering the employees as passive instruments. However, there is nothing in the model that assures this obedience whenever these governing mechanisms are human beings rather than machines. At this point, then, the motivational model of March and Simon can be integrated into the homeostatic model. The occasional disobedience or imperfection in the execution of instructions due to motivational constraints can be considered as some sort of internal disturbance or noise in the channels of communications. The channel of correction should consider the motivational aspects of organizational behavior as an important factor in the decision-making process. Furthermore, this model allows for more adaptability to practical business situations since it takes into consideration the human factor with no assumed constraints on its behavior. In other words, it provides sufficient flexibility for a more complete and realistic reflection of practical phenomena. It is also has the virtue of a systematic position for accounting data and accounting techniques in its regulation-information-communication characteristics. Moreover, provision for disturbances, regulation, the $\mathcal{M}$ and non-$\mathcal{M}$ states, and survival makes available to us an operational tool for explaining, analyzing, and deciding about significant problems in the international petroleum industry. These are the reasons why the homeostatic model is chosen from the several alternatives enumerated above.

3.4. *Accounting Data, Accounting Methodology, and the Managerial Decision-Making Process*

In the accounting literature we meet two kinds of reports. Some are merely descriptive, in the sense that they are comprised of what are supposed to be bare facts about the environment of the organization; undistorted or unevaluated information about its internal state with no attempt at analysis or interpretation, leaving such action to the decision-making unit. Other reports are more sophisticated in that they are analytical and interpretative. However, they are still concerned with either the internal or the external state of the organization or both. The first category of reports and statements is the one meant by accounting data proper. In the second category, the descriptive part also belongs to accounting data, but the analytical interpretative part belongs to the managerial decision-making unit that is supposed to exercise its power and ability to protect the organization from any disturbances. It is the judgment of management built on the descriptive accounting information, mainly accounting data. This is the context in which accounting data is being used hereafter. It is the descriptive, supposedly more objective cost and financial information about the internal or the external state of the organization, or about both. This follows from the structural pattern of our model which is our basic frame of reference. In the model we found that information about disturbances is transmitted to the regulator, R, the agent of the decision-making unit, for action which may include analysis through T, the table that gives outcomes. The important thing to observe in this model, as far as information is concerned, is the separation involved between information as such and interpretation and action in an effort to neutralize or minimize the effect of disturbances. The information is channeled to the decision-making unit or its agent for interpretation and action. Thus is our definition of accounting data derived from the structure of the model. Consequently, if we may conclude that analysis and interpretation belong properly to accounting methodology, we find that such a methodology is identified with the managerial decision-making process. From our definition of accounting data and its function in the model, then, does the significance of accounting methodology become clearly defined as one of the fundamental tools of the decision-making unit.

3.4.*A. Accounting Data and the Feedback Circuit*

The model that I have just explained as a relatively more useful tool in organization model construction is well-known in the science of cybernetics. The word cybernetics originated in the United States in 1947 as a name for the study of organization, communication, and control of a system, which is exactly what we are concerned with in this chapter, though from a different perspective. The results of cybernetics research are being used by operation research scientists in their studies of systems dealing with factory control. These scientists were always looking for means and ways to make their systems "responsive". Eddison, Pennycuick, and Rivett explain the problem. They say that the operation research scientists "were trying to create the analogue of a man riding a horse: where the information systems of the two components of the system (the horse and the rider) are put into a very special relation so that one is almost an extension of other".[1] By simulating this, we should think in terms of an organization represented by our model in which R, the decision-making unit, is what we put as management. As we explained before, R is supposed to protect E, the set of essential variables, from disturbances, D. To do so, the model provides for feedback mechanisms to convey to R information about D in order that R takes the necessary measures of protection. Through this mechanism, the two information sub-systems converge as an extension of one another. They continue: "A manager who reviews results at the end of the month, through his cost statement and his reports on the level of machine utilization, rejections, and so on and then holds a meeting to award praise or blame is operating a feedback circuit."[2]

This is another connecting link between accounting data and the organization model. It is a part of the feedback circuit. To operate the organization successfully, to achieve its essential goals, management relies in part upon a complex system of reports and feedbacks, an important and essential part of which are accounting reports and all kinds of financial and cost data. Such reports, which are accounting data in a broad sense, are the tools which make the organization and its model dynamic and responsive. They are the means through which the internal and external states of the organization are conveyed to the decision-making unit in the organization.

The extension of the two systems of information into each other is further strengthened by the links between accounting data and accounting methodology which we have discussed. In the terms of the operation research scientists, the information system of the horse is simulated by the

---

1. R. T. Eddison, K. Pennycuick and B. H. Rivett, *Operational Research in Management* (London: The English Universities Press, 1962), p. 130.
2. *Ibid.*, p. 31.

systems of accounting and financial reporting to the decision-making unit, the rider, whose information system interprets, analyzes, and then decides a course of action utilizing whatever information comes from the horse. It is this structure of interconnected and inter-responsive systems which most nearly satisfies the biological description of the organization which we have offered. The process of the ideal transmission of information from one element of the organization to another frees each element to perform its individual function and to contribute thereby to the achievement of the organism's ultimate goal, survival.

CHAPTER IV

Accounting Contribution to the Survival of the Organization

IN ORDER to establish the significance of income determination in relation to the existence and viability of an organization, let us apply the model we have developed in Chapter III to the international petroleum industry.

It will assist in the portrayal and explanation of the disturbances that exist and affect the destiny of business organizations belonging to this international industry. In other words, the homeostatic organization model is utilized as an operational tool to establish the descriptive and functional nature of such disturbances, to provide evidence substantiating the existence and significance of such disturbances, and to clarify the role that accounting in general and accounting income determination in particular play in counteractions against such disturbances. Accounting data and accounting techniques, being an essential communication-information link for effective regulation of such organizations, could effectively serve the objectives of these organizations and contribute positively to their viability and survival in a turbulent environment, provided such accounting data and techniques are utilized in a more objective and unbiased manner. The contribution of the accounting discipline to the survival of these organizations depends heavily on its ability to provide a more objective solution to the income determination question in this industry. It depends on its ability to provide a neutral value for such income. Such a supposedly unbiased and neutral answer within a given frame of reference would be the outcome of this study.

Hence the environmental disturbances in the international oil industry are the subject of this chapter. To provide for effective regulation against such disturbances, accounting has something to say both in the form of income determination and in the form of survival-oriented accounting reporting and disclosure.

4.1. Security and Survival

We have seen that, for our purposes, the fundamental goal of the organization is survival. R. Harré has elaborated on this in his *Introduction to the Logic of the Sciences:*

> The needs which have produced sciences are not something new that suddenly inspired exceptional people to undertake a new kind of activity. They are indeed ordinary, springing from the general insecurity of human life. Security is obtained by first knowing the facts, knowing what the situation is in which we find ourselves and secondly knowing how to manipulate it to our advantage. Knowing how to manipulate our environment to our own advantage gives us the power upon which our general security can be based.[1]

Such power could be obtained through generalizations concerning the information which is supplied about the world and by further predictions, but it is amplified by analyzing the reasons underlying observed phenomena.

The writings of Professor Harré and others in the field of the logic of the sciences have not been oriented toward organization or accounting theory or social sciences in general. The subjects of their studies are the natural sciences. However, there is no reason why we cannot adopt the logic of the natural sciences if that proves helpful in promoting better understanding of the workings of organizations.

The assumption that security and survival are fundamental to the organization suggests that organizational decisions contribute either positively or negatively to this goal in varying degrees. In order to make such decisions, we must first analyze the organization and its environment. This is done in two steps. The first explains in abstract terms the organization's internal and external states; i.e. its internal and external environment. The second will be an application of this abstract analysis to the international petroleum industry. The evidence will be utilized or manipulated as a guide

---

1. R. Harré, *An Introduction to the Logic of the Sciences* (London: Macmillan, 1960), p. 41.

to organizational decisions compatible with the security and survival of an international petroleum organization.

4.2. *The Environment of an Organization: A Symbolic Formulation*

An organization does not live in a vacuum. It affects and is affected by a number of disturbances, hereafter called environmental variables, relating either to its internal state of affairs or to the external state of affairs. Two of such variables affect organizational decisions internally: the human factor and the material factor. In the following equations, the employees shall be symbolized by the letter P and the materials by the letter M. There are other variables related to the organization's external state of affairs which also have a significant effect on the organizational decisions. These external variables include all variables that have a possible effect upon organizational decisions but which do not belong to its internal environment.[1] The organization's external environment might be described in terms of its owners, the general public; the other organizations in the same industry; the government or governments which are related to the organization; the national and world economy; and, finally, technology with all its ramifications.[2] This grouping of variables is so extensive that there is nothing remaining which cannot be subsumed under one or another variable.

In sequence, we may symbolize these variables by the letters (A, B, C, G, Y, and F). The security and survival of the organization, symbolized by the letter V, is taken to be a function of the essential variables E referred to above; whereas such a set of variables is a function of the environmental variables D. In formulae, the relationships may be expressed thus: $V = V(E)$ and $E = E(P, M), (A, B, C, G, Y, F)$. If ($P, M$) are symbolized by the letter (I) and (A, B, C, G, Y, F) are symbolized by the letter (X), then,

$$E = R(I, X)$$

Substituting D for (I, X), we have $E = K(D)$.

---

1. George R. Terry, *op. cit.*, p. 5.
2. *Ibid.*, p. 44.

4.2. A. Two Subsets of Essential and Environmental Variables

So far, we have indicated that the survival of the organization ($\mathcal{V}$) depends upon the essential variables ($\mathcal{E}$) where E is a function of the environment variables ($\mathcal{D}$).

Only one portion of the essential variables (E) needs protection through counteraction by accounting decisions whenever disturbances from ($\mathcal{D}$) are transmitted to $\mathcal{E}$. Similarly, not all disturbances are counteracted by accounting decisions but rather only a portion thereof. Our concern is directed, then, only to a subset *(e)* of the essential variables and another *(d)* of the environmental variables will be referred to by letters *(p, m, a, b, c, y, g, f)* as against the set *($\mathcal{P}$, $\mathcal{M}$, $\mathcal{A}$, $\mathcal{B}$, $\mathcal{C}$, $\mathcal{T}$, $\mathcal{Y}$, $\mathcal{G}$,)*.

Determination of the components of the set of essential variables is a prerequisite to an aggregative treatment of an organization. It is not so for a partial examination such as the one we are concerned with in this dissertation. Hence, only that subset *(e)* which is affected by the subset of disturbance *($\mathcal{D}$)* needs to be at least partially known. In context of an accounting analysis, such subset *(e)* necessarily relates to financial matters. The rate of return on investment *(t)*, dividend per share *(s)*, and the level of wages and salaries *(w)* are among the most prominent portions of the subset *(e)* of the essential variables. We shall assume that, for our purposes, the subset *(e)* is composed of *(t, s, and w)*.

Furthermore, since survival ($\mathcal{V}$) is a function of $\mathcal{E}$, we shall assume that the other subsets of $\mathcal{E}$ are kept constant, so that V depends upon *(e)* while other things are being equal. For this purpose survival is referred to by the letter *(v)*.

Moreover, since world economy, referred to by the letter $\mathcal{Y}$, and technology, referred by the letter $\mathcal{F}$, do not seem to affect our subset *(e)* in a manner that can be even partially counteracted by an accounting decision, they are not considered in the reformulation of our original equations which follows.

$$v = v\,(e) \qquad\qquad e = e(p, m),\, (a, b, c, g).$$

If *(p, m)* are symbolized by the letter *i* and *(a, b, c, g)* are symbolized by the letter *u*, then

$$e = r\,(i, u)$$

Substituting i for (i, u), we have

$$e = k\,(i)$$

4.2. B. Income and Survival

An oversimplification underlies the symbolic formulation of the relationships between survival and the essential and environmental variables presented above in this chapter. This simplification relates to the assumed behavior of the environmental variables. It should be observed that, although e is a function of i, the level of values that e can take in order to function as a positive contributor to survival must be kept within the limits of the state $\mathcal{M}$. This desirable level of values is determined in partial independence of the environmental variables. In other words, another outside factor exists and relates to the determination of the desirable levels. One of these desirable levels is postulated to be the most desirable among such levels. It is the one determined through the application of the accounting theory of the neutral value of net income. In the meantime the values that (i), the subset of the environmental variables, may take are the basic consideration in the determination of the neutral value of net income. Hence the neutral value level of net income, once determined for the organization, would serve the survival purpose through a certain set of values for the environmental variables.

Should e refer to income as a subset of the essential variables $\mathcal{E}$, then the survival level value of e is given to us by the accounting theory of the neutral value of net income. By definition this value of e is a solution where i takes values that lead to taking this desirable level. Only in this sense, that the equation $e = k\,(i)$ is in a survival state $\mathcal{M}$. In other words, the desirable solution of the equation is given by another equation, the one that determines a neutral value for net income. Hence an equation for the neutral value of net income is needed.

Suppose that the net income is $e = r - c$ and the neutral value of net income is e_i where r takes a value r_i and c takes a value c_i. Then the desirable solution of the equation $e = k(i)$ is given by the equation $e_i = r_i - c_i$.

But the values that r_i and c_i may take are dependent among other things upon a descriptive behavior of the environmental variables. Descriptive behavior is meant to be circumstantial evidence of the direction in which this subset of environmental variables tends to be inclined as net income takes different ranges of values. This circumstantial evidence is postulated to prove that should $\mathcal{R}$ and $\mathcal{C}$ be determined in a certain unbiased manner, the behavior of such a subset of environmental variables would be more in the direction of promoting organizational survival than otherwise. In other words, the behavior of the environmental variables in the basic equation $\mathcal{E} = K(\mathcal{D})$ under varying conditions would lead to varying values for $\mathcal{E}$, hence varying values for its subset e.

Should e take a value other than $e_i = r_i - c_i$, because the behavior of the environment variables, the decision-making unit of the organization would act in one way or another to restore order in the organization. If the organization is to survive, e must always equal $r_i - c_i$, other things being equal. In other words, it is a basic criterion for the decision-making unit in the organization to follow. It is built into the model itself and in its self-regulating mechanism. Only within this context should the symbolically mathematical formulation be viewed.

A more sophisticated mathematical formulation would only divert our attention from elaborating the circumstantial evidence to the behavior of a subset of the environmental variables. This is considered more immediate and consistent with the sequence of the analysis. It is the subject of the following section as the preliminary step toward the determination of r_i and c_i and the neutral value of net income.

4.3. The Organization Defined

"Splitting its World Six Ways is Part of Standard of Jersey's New Plan for Realignment" offers an empirical definition of international petroleum business organization. Jersey Standard covered almost every part of the globe outside the Communist bloc. Its international complex organization was divided into six basic divisions: one for the United States, another for Canada, and a third for the rest of the Western Hemisphere. The fourth division was for North and Western Europe, and part of North and West Africa. The fifth covered the Middle East and the sixth constituted Japan, Australia, South East Asia, India, and East and South Africa.[1] Most of the other international business organizations have similar, though somewhat less complex, international setups in terms of geography. A look at employment and at the value of trade adds to the picture of the world petroleum industry. In his address to the Sixth World Petroleum congress, M. J. Rathbone, President of Jersey Standard said:

---

1. *Business Week*, August 6, 1960, pp. 44–5.

> Petroleum moving between nations is the biggest single item in
> world trade – about 9% of the total. Our industry directly employs
> well over a million people, and indirectly creates employment for
> many millions more.[1]

An international petroleum organization might be a private or government-owned oil company operating on an integrated basis in several countries either directly by itself or through wholly or partially owned subsidiaries. As such, it has production, transportation, refining, marketing, and distribution facilities in many parts of the world, including its homeland. In such a context, the organization is involved in relations with many governments as well as with other petroleum and non-petroleum business organizations. It must be aware of the advances in technology in many fields of science; and it must be familiar with the local economics of many countries and with the world economy as a whole. In addition, its owners, employees, and the public in many different parts of the world must be considered in its organizational decisions. Most of its decisions are financial and are related to prices or costs of petroleum, to revenues from its production, to taxes on its distribution, or to remunerations to employees and partners.

An analysis of such factors provides indicative circumstantial evidence to the significance of an unbiased determination of net income. Such analysis is categorized in the following sub-sections.

4.3. A. Employees (p)

The basic financial interest of the employees of an international petroleum organization is material welfare. Evidence of this can be obtained by comparing an oil producing company blue or white collar worker, manager, or chief executive with those of any other organization in an oil exporting country. The international petroleum organization, to survive, requires as a sub-goal a good standard of living for its employees, particularly because of the obvious high profitability of the petroleum producing business of an international petroleum organization. If the organization is continuously earning more money, the employees believe that they, too, should earn higher wages. The attitude of the employees rises or falls according to the level of the net income of the international petroleum organization.

---

1. Monroe J. Rathbone, President of Standard Oil Co. of New Jersey, *Oil in the Service of Man*, Sixth World Petroleum Congress, Frankfurt/Main, June 19, 1963, p. 1.

Net profits could be understated or overstated even under generally accepted accounting principles. There always will be positive and negative pressures for over- or understatement of net income; many of these pressures come from the international petroleum exporting countries and the international business organizations. But, as far as accounting's contribution in coping with this factor, there seems to be a range of solutions. If the organization's net income could be understated legally, this might be an optimum solution. However, since higher company income is an index of organizational success, satisfying as such some of the aspirations of ambitious personnel, an unbiased neutral value for net income would take care of both considerations in a compromised manner. Consequently, an accounting practice (decision) that is compatible with this sub goal must be a practice that should be followed in order to contribute positively to the organization's survival, other things being equal.

4.3.B. Materials (m)

The "materials" factor in the organization's internal environment is not responsive; in itself it does not have any desires or wishes to express that should be taken into consideration in any accounting decision. Nonetheless, the monetary book values of these materials (assets) are manifestly significant in the international petroleum industry because of their direct effect on the division of profits between the oil companies and the exporting governments. They also affect the tax positions of the organizations at home. Naturally all of this is an outcome of two basic factors; namely, the known and the unknown values of such assets; in other words, the recognized and written monetary values and the omitted unrecognized values of a certain part of them, and the capitalization and the method of expensing related to such assets. A more complete accounting analysis of this problem will be presented in Chapter XI.

An accounting decision compatible with the survival of the organization should give to such assets a value that reflects a more realistic picture of these assets in the form of a more objective evaluation. The basic groups interested in such a process other than the organization itself, are its owners and the tax collectors in the exporting country and at home. To know what is acceptable to them is difficult. However, it is clear that they have opposite desires. This brings us back to the same arena of opposing pressures, this time in assets evaluation and capitalization and expensing policies. We will examine the latter policies in Chapters VIII through X.

The accounting decision concerning any one of such related issues must be one that can accommodate the opposing pressures in a certain position of compromise without prejudice to its basic goal. Such a position has a limit beyond which the organization can no longer survive.

The desires of the owners of the organization, in contrast to the opposing pressure from the government of an exporting country, are major considerations in any accounting decision. For example, in a clear clash of opposing desires, a petroleum organization operating as a foreign interest in an oil exporting country wishes its margin of profits to appear as small as possible so that the share of profit it must, by agreement, return to the exporting country will be as small as possible. The government of the exporting country, on the other hand, wishes the profits of the organization to be assessed at a high level so that its share will be correspondingly greater. So that there may be a satisfactory compromise to solve this conflict, the accounting unit within the organization should offer a value for net income which is demonstrably neutral, that is, wholly objective and undistorted as far as is possible within the uncertainties of the situation. Conflicts of this type arise from biased accounting methods, and, in this potentially dangerous situation, only a more objective accounting method offers a better solution.

4.3.C. The Owners (a)

In considering the factor of ownership, we move to the external environment of the organization. In a typical international petroleum organization, owners are the highest board of directors in its complex system. They command the final word in the affairs of the organization. In our model they resemble our control, C, which tells the regulator, the decision-making unit, certain basic considerations and policies as guide lines for their decisions. Their decisions must involve many factors, such as the diversification of sources of supply and the cooperation with other organizations, for the protection of a common interest. To protect the organization's longrun security and survival they are involved in a multiplicity of bargaining situations. A further important consideration in their continuous effort to protect the organization is the provision of ever-mounting financial requirements to protect their international competitive position. One of the forms of such a consideration is manipulation to keep as much as possible from the profits of operating the petroleum producing concession. This brings us back to the pressures in defining the area of profits. Although the percentage of profit shared is a matter of agreement or tax provision, the actual quantity is an accounting question. Here is a problem of defining revenues rather than costs. It is an inter-organization pricing problem which shall be examined in more detail n Chapter VII. In an integrated system of operations, the lower the prices in one stage, the higher the profits in the second and the lower in the first.

The owners are interested and exercise pressure to the extent that the area of revenues, as far as the producing stage is concerned, is as narrow as possible. The evidence of this can be taken from the controversy over pricing between the Organization of Petroleum Exporting Countries (OPEC) and the international oil companies following the two reductions in the prices of crude oil in February 1959 and August 1960. The uniqueness of the situation arises from the fact that the public accountant would like to certify in prices that are comparable to those that arise in transactions at arm's-length. Whether or not they represent the owners, their goal is to avoid, insofar as possible submission to the owners' pressure. They prefer to certify revenues which produce a neutral value for net income. This, though, does not satisfy the owners' pressure to narrow the area of the profits. It does satisfy the survival objective, since it is bound to reduce to a minimum the opposing pressures of widening such area.

Accordingly, the accounting decision to be taken must have as its basic consideration in this case the quantification of revenues at prices comparable to prices arising from transactions at arm's-length, for this is compatible with the survival of the organization.

4.3. D. The General Public (b)

Because our organization operates in a number of countries, including its home country, its general public is not homogeneous. In the home country the general public is both a consumer of the product of the organization and a potential owner of its stock. The general public, then, has a vital interest in the value of the organization's stock. But its financial information usually disclosed is confined to the balance sheet, the income statement, and, in some cases, the fund statement. The public's interest in these statements is twofold. On the one hand, the monetary quantifications appearing in such statements give them certain leads about the value of the stock; and, on the other hand, the form in which such information is put will give additional leads to the same objective.

We have said that the public of an international petroleum organization is not homogeneous, neither in its interest in the organization nor in its attitude regarding whatever financial information is disclosed; nor in its pressure on the organization and on the government of the host country or countries. The interest of the host general public does not fall into the category of investing in the stock of the organization. The reason is that usually little or none of the stock of the constituent parts of an international petroleum organization is offered in the stock markets of the host countries.

Our most serious concern, however, is the probable existence of a different interest in the financial information. The public attitude in a typical host petroleum producing country is that they are being "exploited" by the "foreigners". In the local newspapers and magazines throughout the Middle East, for example, frequent articles on "exploitation" are published. Such pronouncements are made either by laymen who usually know little about the oil industry in their country, through letters and articles to the editors; or, less frequently, by some informed persons who are not involved in the industry. The essence of the argument quite frequently revolves around the word "exploitation", which is vaguely defined as a kind of disguised robbery. The public, by its nature, is not composed of accountants or of those well-versed in financial matters. In accounting decisions one should start by convincing the public that, under the effective agreements at the date of publishing, the country is not exploited. A simplified set of financial data should be published, substantiated by comments about controversies and certification of its correctness. A well-informed public is far more compatible with the survival of an international petroleum organization. Accordingly, the accounting decision to be made is one of disclosure of material financial and tax happenings in a simplified, well-substantiated manner.

In the typical case, oil is refined and marketed in one country and produced in another. Accordingly, an international petroleum organization might find itself placed with a general public of different categories, unlike its home or "host producing" country public. It is the general public of a petroleum consuming country. Such a public normally is price conscious.

But the pricing of petroleum products for the consumer is affected by a multiplicity of factors, particularly in the international markets. A complex controversial system of crude oil pricing is involved. Such pricing is the most significant factor in the ultimate cost of processing petroleum products. We shall not be concerned here with the complexities of pricing in the international petroleum industry; instead we shall start from the cost of production. Then we have the cost of processing petroleum products or delivering them to the consumer as our starting point. Here we are brought to the point where a reporting and disclosure question is involved. It is a question of whether or not the disclosure of a material occurrence as related to others in the same context is compatible with the survival of the organization. If a price-conscious public is well-informed about the cost of production as related to the final price it is paying and as compared with prices of substitutes, its attitude will be more favorable to the organization. This is particularly true in the case where the net-back to the organization, including the cost of production, is a relatively small fraction of the final payment by the consumer. The difference lies in taxes and levies properly attributed to the consumer and his local government. In many petroleum consuming countries, levies and taxes on petroleum products constitute a large proportion of the final payment by the consumer for a gallon of oil.

It becomes obvious that, in the international oil products market, relevant cost of production figures should be disclosed to the public to add to the factors favorable to the survival of an international petroleum organization. This, in terms of accounting, may not be conventional, but it is derived from the basic objectives of the organization; and it is one of the basic considerations in an accounting decision regarding reporting and disclosure to the general public.

4.3.E. Petroleum and Other Business Organization (c)

Other business organizations, both petroleum and other concerns, are part of the external environment of the organization. They constitute both the local and the international economy.

The relationship between an oil organization and other business organizations in the same industry is quite apparent. On the whole, they produce, refine, ship, and market the same products. They even sell to each other or participate in one stage or another in the industry. The points of contact between the two components of the industry are both competition and cooperation. Although a seeming paradox, such a combination occurs frequently. Two or three companies may own an oil concession, operate it together, and then each company competes with the other in marketing.

Competition of this sort is clearly not "free competition". A less frequent occasion of such a combination is where an oil company has more crude resources than its marketing capabilities. Often such a company prefers to dispose of its surplus crude through some sort of partnership with another organization, from production through delivery to the ultimate consumer, and share all expenses and profits through all the stages. In the normal case, the stockholders of a corporation are from the general public; a general accounting report is considered by a board of directors where careful examination of accounting and financial reports takes place. Usually, managerial types of accounting reports are used.

Accordingly, we have two occasions for consideration of accounting decision-making. The first is managerial accounting reporting and the other might be called "participation accounting reporting". We have assumed that the organization and its management have one dominating objective, namely, the survival of the organization. Thus, managerial accounting reports, to be compatible with the basic managerial objective, should always put among the data or accounting decisions recommended to management all the alternatives with some survival oriented considerations. No contradiction or particular analysis should take place, since any avoidance of such presentation might lead to a managerial decision unfavorable to organizational survival. This adds one more factor to managerial decision-making, and that is a review of other relevant accounting decisions to allow for reservations on the managerial decision lest it contradict some underlying accounting decision unknown to the management. If discovered, this could be harmful in the sense that those interested in the organization will lose confidence in it. Sound decision-making depends, essentially, on presentation of alternatives and evaluation of such alternatives in an aggregate context that takes into consideration all foreseeable effects and consequences. Occasions of contradiction do occur in all organizations due to the failure in communicating relevant information at the right time. Information and communication processes are critical to the survival of the organization.

The relationship of the organization with management, the public and other organizations is one of communication of information considered relevant to a decision or critical to the survival of the organization. Only in this case are such factors related to accounting decision-making. They, in fact, relate to the design of the accounting and accounting-reporting system and to the specification of such a system.

Two significant categories of other organizations exist. The first is organizations that produce substitutes for petroleum, such as coal and other energy sources. The second is credit institutions that partially finance part of the investment requirements of the petroleum industry. The first category, in essence, is only another element of competition; hence little accounting contribution could be made in this direction. Credit institutions are different, for they need and use accounting information. However, their requirements are more or less similar to those of potential investors; accordingly, material consistent information must be supplied to them.

4.3. F. The Consideration of Governments (g)

There are five significant factors in the organization's relationship to governments: the three governments of the host producing, host consuming, and home countries in addition to groups of host governments, whether producing or consuming. To be able to assess the significance of accounting decision-making in this context, we should know the various financial interests involved, their effect on the survival of the organization, and how accounting can serve this goal under these different conditions. Since we have at least five topics to deal with we shall arrange the discussion according to the following categories.

1. *The government of the host producing country*
   Usually, the relationship between a petroleum business organization and the government of a host petroleum producing country is governed by two important documents: the concession agreement and the contract or contracts agreements and supplements that specify the rights and obligations of the oil business organization and the government of the host producing country. In the typical case, the concession agreement specifies bonuses and other payments measured in terms of fixed monetary figures per unit of production or a percentage of the sales price of the unit. None of these provisions present any significant consideration for an accounting decision.
   The provisions of any income tax law, no matter how precise, involve different interpretations. Since they usually deal with taxable income and, subsequently, with revenues and allowable and disallowable expenses, such items in the accounting of taxes to the government present certain controversies. This brings us back to pressures for distorting the value of

net income. The organization is trying to avoid taxes as much as possible, while governments' tax agents are inclined to do the opposite within the provisions of the tax law. Although there are certain allowables and disallowables which are clearly identified, often we find that the tax law leaves much for interpretation. A tax attorney will give many ways of calculating expenses. The tax agent might pick one most favorable to the government and the company representative one favorable to his company. To resolve controversies, only accounting methods which lead to a relatively undistorted value for net income should be used.

Starting with the premise that financial relations with a host producing government are most critical to the survival of the organization, a more objective system of financial and cost petroleum accounting is believed to be most compatible. With the survival of the petroleum business organization. With the grouping of governments, such as the Organization of Petroleum Exporting Countries, the whole international petroleum industry is at stake. The crux of the problems involved between OPEC and the oil companies is financial. Thus it is easy to see the significance of accounting methodology in government – company relationships.

Accounting for the determination of net income still has an extremely significant effect on the trend of relations between international petroleum business organizations and the governments of the host producing countries. Since the early 1950s the 50–50 formula of profit sharing has been in effect in the Middle East. The formula has been under examination by many host governments. Currently, many of these host governments believe it is too favorable to the integrated oil companies. Those who hold these judgments of great international significance look to accounting for a satisfactory and equitable value for net income. Several studies have been made to determine the rate of return on investment in the international petroleum industry, but the controversy continues to grow. Evaluation of assets and determination of net income are basic to any study of the rate of return. Accounting should and can provide the answers.

2. *The government of the home country of a petroleum business organization*
    The relationship between the government of the home country and an international petroleum business organization can be seen from three sides. First, the petroleum business organization, with all its

constituents, is a tax payer, although certain parts of an international petroleum organization may not be subject to the income tax laws of the home country. Usually, though, most of the constituents of the organization are subject to the United States income tax regulations or similar regulations in other countries, with tax credits for foreign taxes involved. Political considerations, such as commanding sources of supply, represent the second aspect. The third side, the significance of which is continuously increasing, is the home government as a partner (stock-holder) in the international petroleum organization. It appoints directors and has a legitimate financial interest in the operations. The home country's government here is similar to the owners. However, the home government as a tax collector has a different status. The most important consideration here is tax credit and the consequences with accounting methods.

The summary of the tax credit question

J. E. Hartshorn, in his book, *Oil Companies and Governments*, writes, "The international sweep of this industry (the international oil industry) does not absolve it from living with governments, as every other industry has to; it only introduces the complication, which can have advantages but has disadvantages as well, of living with more governments than one."[1] Primary in every such relationship with individual governments is the oil industry's role as a tax payer of each country of which it is a commercial citizen.[2] Regarding the importance of the tax treatment in the home country, Hartshorn believes "the tax treatment of oil profits in the country where any international company has its headquarters is likely to condition its industrial strategy all over the world".[3] The tax system at home and the treatment it applies to taxes paid abroad set the basic frame of reference for each oil company. In the United States, Britain, and Europe, headquarters of the largest international companies, taxes paid abroad can be set against tax liabilities at home and royalties paid abroad are excluded from tax consideration as costs of doing business.[4]

There is, then, an inherent relationship between the tax credit to be obtained and the 50–50 formula. In the American case, the depletion

1. J. E. Hartshorn, *op. cit.*, chapter xii.
2. *Ibid.*, p. 175.
3. *Ibid.*
4. *Ibid.*

allowance as a percentage of gross income is 27½ %.[1] Whatever tax credit or percentage depletion allowance is to be allowed is definitely affected by the way the 50–50 formula is applied. It is a 50–50 of taxable net income. Accordingly, the tax credit and depletion allowance problems are, in essence, part of the problem of income determination. Thus the accounting decision to be made does not differ from the one to be made as far as the relationship with a host government is concerned from the profit-sharing tax angle.

3. *The government of a consuming country*
The governments of the petroleum consuming countries have been so occupied with their energy policies that little attention is paid to financial or accounting matters. Input prices have been under examination by many governments. Other governments are conscious of the fact that some oil subsidiaries are almost always in the red. However, since the taxes on such subsidiaries are a minor source of their revenues, the problem is not so acute. The governments have a guaranteed tax through custom duties and consumer levies on petroleum and its products. Yet, accounting plays an insignificant part in energy policies of these countries, which are dominantly affected by input prices on the one hand and nationalistic attitudes on the other. None of these factors are substantially accounting problems.

4. *Groupings of consuming governments*
Among the several economic and energy associations of some oil consuming countries, the Organization for Economic Cooperation and Development has been particularly active in the field of petroleum economics. The Common Market is another that has contributed, similarly, but from a different perspective. However, their common dominating interest, as energy consumers, is the free flow of oil at prices consistent with its future development, without jeopardizing the generation of sufficient capital for the future development of energy resources.[2]

It has been rumored that some of these countries are considering the formulation of an Organization for the Petroleum Importing

---

1. *Oil Recent Developments in the OEEC Area*, The Oil Committee, The Organization for European Economic Cooperation, Paris, 1961, p. 15.
2. *Ibid.*, p. 133.

Countries (OPIC) as a counterpart for OPEC. Although there has been no significant sign of such a trend, such an organization is possible, and, in the case of its creation, sound accounting practices will be required to substantiate a number of arguments related to OPEC issues and resolutions. Costing and profit sharing formulas and agreements between the parties concerned require accounting criteria for substantiation. Accounting decision-making involves realism along with logically defensible methodology. It involves being more objective under conditions of uncertainty and incomplete information.

5. *Grouping of host producing countries' governments*
The governments of the petroleum exporting countries have always felt some weakness in their bargaining power with regard to the international integrated oil companies, primarily because of their implicit unity and ability to use the crude oil sources of one country in cases involving differences with another country. This is particularly true because of the great dependence of these countries on oil revenues. There are other reasons, nationalistic and otherwise, behind the movement toward unity on the part of the petroleum producing countries. Two movements have gained momentum. The first was the organization by the Arab League of a series of annual Arab Petroleum Congresses, of which the first was held in Cairo in 1959, the second in Beirut, the third in Alexandria in 1961, the fourth in Beirut in November 1963 and the fifth in Cairo in March 1965. A more serious attempt to organize the producing countries was the creation, in August 1960 of OPEC. The relationship of the Organization of the Congress was explained by Sheikh Abdullah Al-Tariki when he said that, while the Congress was a forum of public opinion on oil matters, OPEC was the forum for the governments where vitally important matters, such as prices and proration and uniform accounting systems, could be discussed. So far only prices and a few accounting and tax questions have been raised by OPEC.

The problem facing us, then, in our analysis of accounting decision-making, is the significance of such decisions so far as the OPEC demands and resolutions are concerned and the extent of their effect on the survival of an international business organization. Our starting premise here is the potential power of the Organization to enact decisions and enforce them. These decisions might contribute negatively to the survival of the international petroleum business organizations, at least in the long run. Thus, it does not mean cutting off the service to the consumer or any similar political action; it is, rather, a potential change in the form of the service that might eliminate the role of an integrated oil company. There have been occasions where prominent leaders in the international oil industry gave indications of such potential dangers. In a paper submitted to the Third Arab Petroleum Congress by the National Italian Oil Company (ENI), the group owned by the Italian Government, it was stated, "The consuming countries should get together with the producing countries and conclude long-term supply contracts with them directly, thereby to that extent excluding the integrated groups from the business altogether."[1]

Among the many resolutions that OPEC has adopted, two are most relevant to accounting and tax decision-making on the part of the international oil companies in addition to being themselves interesting problems for accounting analysis. Resolutions IV. 34 and IV. 33, adopted in the Fourth Conference held in Geneva, 5 – 8 April 1962, are only the beginning of a revision of the accounting practices used by the international oil companies. They are reproduced here for reference to survival and accounting in the international petroleum industry.

Resolution IV. 33 reads as follows:

The conference, considering
1. That the companies enjoying in Member Countries the right of extracting petroleum which is a wasting asset should, in conformity with the principle recognized and the practice observed generally in the world, compensate the Countries for the intrinsic value of such petroleum altogether apart from their obligations falling under the heading of income tax;
2. That under the arrangements at present in force between the Member Countries and the Oil Companies in general no compensation is paid for the intrinsic value of petroleum royalty or stated payment commitments being treated as credits against income tax liabilities;
3. That the Member Countries' right to receive compensation for the intrinsic value of petroleum is incontestable;

1. B. A. C. Sweet-Escott, "National and Social Aspects of an International Industry", *The Oil Industry Tomorrow*, Report of the Summer Meeting of the Institute of Petroleum, M. J. Wells, editor, Institute of Petroleum, London, 1962, p. 133.

RECOMMENDS

That each Member Country affected should approach the Company or Companies concerned with a view to working out a formula where under royalty payments shall be fixed at a uniform rate which Members consider equitable and shall not be treated as a credit against income tax liability.[1]

Resolution IV. 34.

The conference considering

1. That neither the Members nor the Companies operating in their countries participate in the world wide marketing operations of the Oil Companies;

2. That the bulk of the crude oil produced by the Operating Companies is marketed through their parents or parent affiliates with no brokerage charges being incurred;

3. That one of the Member Countries makes no contribution whatsoever to the selling expenses of the Oil Companies;

RECOMMENDS

That the Member Countries affected should take measures to eliminate any contribution to the marketing expenses of the Companies concerned.[2]

Behind those two resolutions lies an accounting theory of great significance to the construction of sound accounting methodology. They are questions of asset valuation and expense determination. Expressions of wasting assets, intrinsic value, and participation in marketing operations are distinctive accounting concepts, so critical in the construction of the theory of accounting.

4.4. Conclusion

The present chapter has been devoted to seeking occasions, in the internal and external environments of a petroleum business organization, for an accounting decision. Such occasions are varied because of their relevance to the organization's basic goal of survival. If a more objective analysis of

---

1. Resolutions adopted at the Conference of the Organization of the Petroleum Exporting Countries, Fourth Conference, April 1962 (first session), p. 47.
2.*Ibid.*, p. 48.

outstanding problems is ever to dominate in bargaining situations, solutions of these problems can come at least partially from accounting. Nevertheless, whatever contributions accounting can make in this area definitely and paradoxically add to the bargaining power of both sides. Accounting offers unbiased and objective answers, extremely valuable considerations in any managerial decisions of oil companies. Thus, the service of accounting to management and, subsequently, its contribution to the survival of the international oil companies is obvious.

We thereby conclude the construction and application of the homeostatic model to the international petroleum industry, using this model as a substitute for the conventional accounting entity concept. In other words, the groundwork for the examination of the conventional accounting concepts and premises in light of the organization model and the goals and sub-goals inherent in it is already established. Such examination would be the first step in arriving at more objective accounting recognition and measurement techniques to provide for a less distorted and a relatively unbiased accounting income determination. This examination of conventional basic accounting premises will take place in the following chapter.

CHAPTER V

The Organization Model and the Basic Premises of Accounting Theory

FOR THE PURPOSES of our study we shall assume that accounting theory is part of the general organization theory. It is part of the information, communication, and decision-making subsystems of the organization model. It affects and is affected by the goal and the sub-goals of the organization, contributing substantially to the premises of managerial decisions critical to the survival of the organization. Accounting commands a great many means – methods, practices, principles, concepts, and standards – that can be utilized in the process of goal-achievement carried out by the decision-making unit, or units, of the organization. In such a process a multiplicity of considerations derived from the internal and external environments of the organization affects the choice of the means, to the extent that the choice of a certain set of means itself must be compatible with the survival of the organization, for it must provide management with the necessary data derived with such considerations in mind. The process of choice, though, is the last thing to be considered in this study. First we must know the means and must assess their contribution to the set of goals which have been discussed in Chapter IV.

We have a basic goal, survival, and a set of considerations, sub-goals, derived from the internal and external environment of the organization. Such sub-goals, which are compatible with the survival of the organization, are used as one set of criteria to be applied in the choice of the accounting methods utilized by the organization, the accounting decision, in the preparation of data used as one of the premises in the decision-making process es of the organization. Often accounting must provide certain explanatory statements and figures which reflect potential positions to be taken by other partners in business dealings. Such positions can be incompatible with the survival of the organization. The contribution of accounting in such cases is found in its ability to communicate to management an explanatory version of the facts so that they may be manipulated to achieve the organization's goals. In other words, accounting either recommends a course of action in financial accounting, and tax matters, or it provides a description of a certain set of facts relevant to factors in its environment in order to facilitate a managerial decision. Such a recommended course of action in accounting matters has definite bearing on the final managerial decision to be taken by the organization.

5.1. Definition of Accounting

I have made several assumptions about the functions of accounting. I should like to substantiate my position by examining the conventional definitions and concepts of accounting. Through this examination, and criticism, of the conventional concepts and goals of accounting I shall define and defend my position.

The American Institute of Certified Public Accountants (AICPA) Committee on Terminology finds that "accounting is the art of recording, classifying, summarizing in a significant manner and in terms of money, transactions and events which are in part at least of a financial character and interpreting the results thereof".[1]

The American Accounting Association defined accounting in terms of defining its functions. The 1957 Committee on Accounting Concepts and Standards of this Association stated that "the primary function of accounting is to accumulate and communicate information essential to an understanding of the activities of an enterprise, whether large or small, corporate or non-corporate, profit or non-profit, public or private".[2] The Committee then added that "to accomplish this function most effectively accounting must develop within a definite framework of concepts and standards".[3] The Committee, however, directed itself to "general purpose reports to stockholders and others

---

1. American Institute of CPAs, *Accounting Terminology Bulletin*, no. 1, *Review and Resumé* (New York, 1953).
2. American Accounting Association, *Accounting and Reporting Standards for Corporate Financial Statements and Preceding Statements and Supplements* (Columbus, Ohio, 1957), p. 1.
3. *Ibid.*

interested in corporate business enterprise".[1]

Since we moved from the general definition to specific functions, we might clarify the picture by adding Paton's views to the analysis. He says that:

> In a broad sense accounting has one primary function: facilitating the administration of economic activity. This function has two closely related phases: 1. measuring and arraying economic data; 2. communicating the results of this process to interested parties.[2]

The statements of the AICPA and the American Accounting Association, together with Paton's specifications of functions, are representative of one line of approach to the problems involved in constructing a theory of accounting. The AICPA definition emphasizes the fact that a large portion of the accounting work is in the observation and recording of data. Nevertheless, this is only one step toward the making of an accounting or a managerial decision. Hence such a definition avoids completely the commitment of the accountant to take a certain course of action, if only to choose one accounting method over another. It further avoids recognition of accounting as a service tool to management. In its logical extreme it reduces accounting to a mere collection of financial data being interpreted as a matter of opinion, or perhaps personal judgment of the accountant. As such it treats accounting completely in isolation. Nevertheless, a few bricks can be taken from this definition to be used in the construction of accounting theory built from facts and leading to the utilization of such facts in serving the goals of the organization. To know the facts we have to provide for "recording" transactions and events and having a certain objective "interpretation" would help in the utilization and decision-making process of the organization.

Such defects are not so apparent in the American Accounting Association (AAA) definition of accounting functions. Although the AAA Committee does not commit itself to accounting being an art, it does not say that accounting is a science, either. However, implicit in the minds of those who issued the statement is "a definite framework of concepts and standards"; a definite theory, we might say. Thus its approach is more theoretical, and more rational.

Aside from the science – art controversy, the AAA hits an important

---

1. *Ibid.*
2. Rufus Wixon and Walter G. Kell, *Accountant's Handbook* (New York: The Ronald Press Co., 1957), p. 1.

characteristic of accounting as it is today and has been since the time the first account was made, namely, the accumulation and communication of information. It was this characteristic which was the fundamental organizational force in our model. An "understanding of the activities of the enterprise" is not the only purpose for which accounting accumulates and communicates information, and one must choose one accounting method over another, according to the specific needs of the organization. Often such decisions are made in organizations with no rational criteria to judge their effectiveness in serving the organization's cause. Both the AICPA and the AAA statements provide many alternatives to choose from, but in most cases these lack the coherence and consistency required in any body of theory. However, the AAA statement is rich in coherent concepts which may contribute to a more integrated theory of accounting. Indeed, the only substantial criticism that can be directed to the AAA statement concerns its lack of integration and the limited scope of its propositions, particularly with regard to the services which accounting does provide. W. A. Paton's delineation of the functions of accounting really falls within the AAA statement except for its indication to facilitating the administration of economic activity, which is admittedly different from the understanding of the enterprise activities.

This line of approach is thought to be representative of the conventional theoretical development of accounting in a very concise form. Two objectives are in mind. The first is to look to accounting clearly in a larger environment rather that in isolation or within the limits of the business entity, conventionally defined. The integration of accounting theory with organization theory is believed to achieve this objective and provides us with a framework within which we can achieve the second objective. The detailed evaluation of the conventional accounting income determination theory within a particular industry represents the ultimate objective of this thesis. In our logical construction such an objective comes next to the one we have just cited, since the integration with organization theory is a prerequisite to the integration and evaluation of the conventional accounting theory itself. Accordingly, our second objective is directed to the unifying and integrating of the many concepts and standards into one logical structure. We shall evaluate simultaneously on the basis of rational criteria.

5.2. Toward Income Determination

In Chapter IV and in the first portion of this chapter, we have seen that the accounting contribution to the organization's cause is achieved through two basic steps. The first is survival-oriented accounting reporting and disclosure, and the second is a more objective, unbiased periodic income determination. It is time now to narrow our examination of oil accounting premises and techniques to those related partially or totally to income determination only. This is the basic objective of the book. Leaving out a more detailed examination of survival-oriented accounting reporting and disclosure in the international petroleum industry should not reflect a lack of significance in the role that improved reporting and disclosure might play in providing a more favorable survival environment. Such examination is left out at this stage only because it does not have a material effect on income determination as such, though the disclosure of survival-oriented income data is in itself significant. To prepare the ground for a more rational income determination in the international petroleum industry the following definitions and basic accounting premises must be examined.

5.2. A. Costs Attach

In *An Introduction to Corporate Accounting Standards*, W. A. Paton and A. C. Littleton write, "Since specific costs express significant parts of total effort expended in producing and selling of a commodity or service, they may be assembled by operating divisions, product parts on time intervals, as if they had the power, like their physical counterparts, of cohering in groups."[1] Further they add, " It is a basic concept of accounting that costs can be marshalled into new groups that possess real significance."[2]

In accounting generally and in cost accounting particularly, to find out what costs have been incurred you face the problem of cost allocation. In the process of transforming factors of production from one form to the other a bit of every factor is regrouped with a bit of other factors to make up the new form. This is a fact in the manufacturing and processing industries and even in purely commercial enterprises. So that such facts may be usable in financial interpretation and accounting decision-making, they should be reflected in terms of monetary units. Otherwise only the physical regrouping is apparent. Accordingly, the cost accounting regrouping of "cost" is derived essentially from the physical regrouping. It is the physical fact in another form more readily usable in the service of the organization cause. We should

---

1. Paton and Littleton, *op. cit.*, p. lx.
2. "A tentative statement of accounting principles underlying corporate financial statements", *The Accounting Review*, June 1956.

not hesitate to speak of facts simply because we do not have natural physical means of measuring them. Conceptual measurement, direct or indirect, monetary or otherwise, is quite as good, if it is derived from the physical fact. The only condition required here is that the financial picture must be approaching the physical picture in all its measurements, if it can not be an exact measurement. Approaching "limit" values are used in mathematics, particularly in calculus and analytic geometry, which are considered as one of the most essential tools of scientific research.

> A variable X approaches a constant as a limit if $(x - a)$ becomes and remains less than any chosen positive constant. The notation $X \longrightarrow$ means 'x approaches a as a limit'.[1]

Such is the definition of a limit value. It means that "in many cases the variable cannot be permitted to become equal to its limit".[2]

This is a good hint we might borrow from mathematics and adapt to our accounting purposes. Adaptation in this case means a slightly different definition of the "limit" concept. Exact measurement of accounting data is impossible or unattainable, at times, because of environment reasons. In such cases and insofar as the measured value of an accounting datum C approaches the exact value of datum C_1, it is taken to be a satisfactory substitute for practical purposes. This is our definition of the accounting "limit" value concept. Hence the reflection of the regrouped physical picture by means of the reallocated cost picture does not have to be an exact replica of the original. To satisfy the accounting definition of the limit concept, the replica (costs reallocated) is only allowed to approach the original. Between the limit values (the original physical picture) and the regrouped costs lies some arbitrariness in accounting measurement. Yet this is not unique, for it is to be found in other disciplines.

This is the logic that underlies the cost allocation methodology in accounting. "Costs attach" is only the effect, while the cause is the physical regrouping of the factors of production. It is a reflection of facts in isolation, as they occurred. This is why such a record of history, though regrouped in the form of apportioned and reallocated cost, should be our starting point in any cost study. Otherwise we go back to a less rational accounting.

---

1. Samuel E. Urner and William B. Orange, *Elements of Mathematical Analysis* (Boston: Ginn and Company, 1950), p. 70.
2. *Ibid.*

5.2.B. Efforts and Accomplishments

> In economics the total "cost of production" is usually conceived of as the price-influencing cost effective at a point of time in a given market area – a cost which includes all elements which the price paid by the purchaser must cover if production is to continue. From this standpoint cost clearly becomes identical with the selling price of the marginal producer and hence includes the elements of marginal profit or income. This is in contrast to the position which is taken by the accountant. Accounting exists primarily as a means of computing a residuum, a balance, the difference between costs (as efforts) and revenues (as accomplishments) for individual enterprises.[1]

This is the matching accounting concept so basic to accounting theory and accounting income determination.

We must avoid imputation and begin by recording whatever financial transactions and events have taken place in a given time period. These are the "efforts" as recorded first in their physical and human picture and as they are then redrawn in periodic monetary measurement (or remeasurement). All this is supposed to reflect a realistic history of costs. It is a record of whatever "efforts" have been expended, displayed in convenient and manageable terminology.

However, the physical and human activities of the organization, "the efforts", are made to achieve a certain set of goals which determine survival. Among the sub goals is the achievement of a certain income since this is necessary for the survival of the organization, and because it serves also the needs of others affecting the organization from both its internal and external environments. In turn, the serving of such needs subsequently contributes favorably to the survival of the organization. In its achievements and accomplishments, it realizes certain revenues, incurring certain expenses, and acquiring certain assets at the same time. In such a process we find that revenues, assets and expenses are surrounded with recognition and measurement difficulties as will be examined in greater detail, starting from the following chapter. This, nevertheless, is in spite of the fact that we do not presume a precise exactness in measurement. We only require somewhat more objectivity and rationality in such recognition and measurement of accounting data, still in the accounting "limit" value sense.

Since the accomplishments have been disposed of at "limit" values higher

---

1. Paton and Littleton, *op. cit.*, pp. 15–6.

than the original, realistic, historical "limit" values of the efforts, a certain residuum is realized. The more the efforts expended approach their limit values, and the more the accomplishments approach their limit values, the more we approach the limit value of net income. Accordingly, the neutral value of net income is dependent on the limit value of costs (efforts) and the limit values of revenues (accomplishments). Methods of determining such limit values will be examined in the next few chapters starting with a representative picture of the present techniques through which income is currently determined. This picture will be portrayed in the following chapter and used as a point of departure for developing the more rational techniques.

5.3. The Fund Theory

A concise statement given by Paton and Littleton indicates the necessity of the business entity concept in accounting thought. They say: "Because accounting and financial statements relate to business enterprise rather than to owners, revenues and costs are defined in terms of changes in enterprise assets rather than as increases or decreases in proprietorship."[1] This is a rejection of the proprietary theory in accounting. The business entity theory itself is also rejected by the author of the fund theory because of "personalization" involved in its application.[2] Instead he develops the concept of a fund. William J. Vatter finds it superior to both the proprietary and entity theory because it can serve "as a basis for accounting that is devoid of personal implications".[3] It is worth mentioning that Vatter's use of the word "fund" is related to its use in governmental and institutional accounting as "a unit of operations or center of interest".

Since they constitute available alternatives, a word should be said as to whether or not there is a contradiction between the fund theory and the organization model developed in this thesis. Although the general organization model is admittedly biological in structure, it is really devoid of personalization. Because the owners of the organization are only one among many other factors in its environment, there is no fear of their being infected by "personal analogies", and the "separation of management from ownership" is readily apparent. At the same time the model's structure is

---

1. *Ibid.*, p.7..
2. William J. Vatter, *The Fund Theory of Accounting and Its Implications for Financial Reports* (Chicago: The University of Chicago Press, 1957), p. 57.
3. *Ibid.*, Chapter 1.

designed with the "manifold use of accounting data" in mind. These were the main objections against the entity theory and they do not seem to apply to our organization model. Furthermore, objectivity is one of the basic criteria around which the model is built, to the extent that an accusation of arbitrariness or lack of objectivity can be largely ruled out.

Nevertheless, there is at least one clear area of difference between the fund theory and the organization model. Vatter recommends the abandonment of "the notion of general purpose income statement", and instead the fund theory provides "The Statement of Fund Operations" which is different from the conventional income statement in both form and content. Yet, net income is basic to accounting theory. Hence it is a necessity in serving the goals of the organization. A concept of net income is basic to the survival of the organization, and thus it is an integral part of organization theory.

5.4. The Entity Theory of Consolidated Statements

The business entity theory, then, is an essential part of the conventional accounting theory. The going-concern concept, which is really only an extension of the entity concept, is another essential part of the theory. Paton and Littleton write:

> The assumption that the business entity has continuity of life may be largely one of convenience, since no one can confidently predict the course of events. Yet some degree of continuity is the typical experience even in the midst of insolvency, liquidation and dissolution.[1]

Such is the typical assumption of the conventional "going-concern" concept. "The concept of a going concern is so much a part of the theoretical backbone of modern accounting as to require no extended comment".[2] Such was Moonitz's opinion regarding the extension of the entity theory. Yet, in fact, he greatly extended the conventional concept of the business entity. Implicit in his entity theory, called the "Entity Theory of Consolidated Statements", is a concept of an organization and its environment, particularly part of its external environment, as in the special case of a holding company. Moonitz states that "the assumption that consolidated statements are best fitted to reflect, on the accounting level, the affairs of an entity composed of a group

---

1. Paton and Littleton, *op. cit.*, p. 9.
2. Maurice Moonitz, *The Entity Theory of Consolidated Statements* (Brooklyn: The Foundation Press, 1951), p. 18.

of closely affiliated companies was based upon an appeal to the historical circumstances shaping their adoption and growth".[1] This statement reflects the close association between the general organization model and the entity theory of consolidated statements. It is an association in the common goal of looking to realities and developing theories devoid of legal restrictions. The model thus accommodates the "affiliated" companies as well as a single company. Furthermore, it satisfies the condition of the Moonitz entity theory that "a coherent theory capable not merely of rationalizing some the practices already prevalent but competent to solve new problems as they arise, must be based on rigorous single-minded attention to the one function which can be performed by consolidated statements better than any other known accounting device".[2])

It does so by accommodating consolidation and by being flexible enough to be capable of rationalizing prevalent accounting practices. Thus, the organization model facilities research because of its flexibility in facing new problems and solving them, and because of its scientific approach toward existing problems. In this, it may be considered an extension of the business entity theory in general and the consolidated statement entity theory in particular. While the latter theory accommodated affiliation, accounting theory, built on the organization model, adds to this accommodation a multiplicity of other factors in the organization's external environment.

5.5. *Conclusions*

We have demonstrated in this chapter the connecting link between our line of accounting theory construction and the conventional underlying accounting premises and theories, particularly the business entity theory and its continuity in the broader sense of a general organization model. This is followed by revenues, costs, and income determination based on premises which are similar to those conventionally accepted, though they arise from, and are therefore modified by, the basic logic of the organization model. Hence the premises are the same, though for a different reason. The line of reasoning starts from the environment of the organization and ends either with an accounting decision to use a certain set of accounting methods or with a managerial decision to utilize accounting data as a part of its premises. Accordingly accounting methods end up with income determination, while

---

1. *Ibid.*, p. 83.
2. *Ibid.*

revenues, costs and assets are determined in the process. There are many different ways (methods) of arriving at revenues, costs, and asset values: only one set of methods leads to a neutral value of net income which is most compatible with organizational survival. Only in this sense, then, an accounting decision is made.

In our study, management is not taken as part of either the internal or external environment of the organization. It is an integral part of the organization itself. The choice of methods and the supply of accounting data to management through its accounting information communication system enables management to choose a certain course of action compatible with the survival of the organization. The internal workings of the organization itself are not dealt with here, for this is the field of managerial accounting with which we are not concerned in this study. It is the third function of the accounting information communication system of the organization that requires special treatment.

From our detailed analysis in Chapter IV we found that, in most cases, the starting point in achieving the cause of an international petroleum organization is a more rationally determined net income, a neutral value of net income. Accordingly, because this is dependent on asset evaluation, revenues, and cost determination, we shall now be concerned with the problems of defining, as realistically and rationally as possible, one of the starting points in the process of achieving the organization's survival state.

CHAPTER VI

Costs and Revenues:
The Present Determination Techniques

WE INDICATED in the previous chapter that the present techniques of determining net income would be stated and used as a point of departure for the development of more objective and impartial techniques of income determination.

It was further stated that the determination of net income is one of the first steps favorable to the survival of the organization to be taken by the management. This is particularly true in the case of an international petroleum organization, especially in connection with some of the critical factors in its internal and external environment. It is critical because the survival of the international industry may be at stake. Accounting provides an objective lead to the most controversial issue in the industry, namely, the rate of return on investment and, subsequently, the profit sharing formulas. As soon as the 50–50 formula was established in the early 1950s, problems of accounting began to show up in the international petroleum industry. "Fifty-fifty of what?"[1] asks *The Economist*. Net income, of course. But whose calculation shall we take? That of the companies, or the governments, or the United States Internal Revenue Service, or similar agencies in other countries? No answer is offered in this paper, for the question is often more political than administrative; however, we shall attempt to show how a more objective and neutral value of net income can be determined in the international petroleum industry.

Accountants are not the only people concerned with costs of oil. Economists, too, have their ideas about the costs of oil and its derivatives.

---

1. *The Economist*, June 29, 1963.

Nevertheless, economic theory in general does not specify the operational methods according to which the total cost of production is calculated. It is interested mainly in total cost and total output and the changes in them in order to make possible a calculation of marginal cost on which economic analysis is built. However, there are some basic economic concepts concerning the elements that enter into the figures of the total cost of production. These concepts lead to some differences between accountants and economists in their approaches of calculation. Thus, in a discussion of fixed costs, W. A. Lewis writes:

> In welfare economics the cost of something is the value to other producers of the resources which are used to produce it; cost is measure by computing what expenses would be saved if production were curtailed and resources released for use elsewhere. This cost differs from cost in the business or accounting sense, which is simply the sum expended on production ...[1]

He further clarifies his statement, saying that "accountants are concerned with original cost but economists with replacement cost".[2] This was the view of an economist regarding the differences between accounting and economic concepts of cost. In Chapter V we examined the accounting cost concept, particularly in its relationship to income determination. Nevertheless, we should mention further that, from the accounting point of view, "it is not necessary to assume a cost theory of value in order to explain the concept that costs cohere. Costs are not marshalled to show value or worth."[3] This is the accounting view as it has been expressed by Paton and Littleton.

With regard to petroleum production cost, we find that Professor Adelman, an economist, accepts the customary grouping of oil and production costs in three categories: exploration, development, and extraction.[4] He generally accepts the responsibility of the accountant "to compute the separate unit costs of the two or more products" in the case of common cost. He says that "this is basically a task for the accountant; the economist has no reason to object".[5] Here the accountant is expected to

---

1. W. A. Lewis, "Overhead costs", *Some Essays in Economic Analysis* (London: George Allen and Unwin Ltd., 1959), p. 9.
2. *Ibid.*, p. 15.
3. Paton and Littleton, *op. cit.*, pp. 13–4.
4. M. A. Adelman, *The Supply and Price of Natural Gas* (Oxford: Basil Blackwell, 1962), p. 3.
5. *Ibid.*, p. 25.

compute unit costs in the case of two or more products under common costs conditions.

Common costs are generally defined by Lawrence L. Vance as "the costs of producing two or more separate (not joint) products with the same facilities at the same time".[1]

So we might assume that he is also expected to compute unit costs in the case of one product. Yet Adelman does reject the allocation of costs in the presence of "joint supply", namely joint costs. The differentiation between common and joint costs is stated again by Lawrence L. Vance as a reflection of difference in tracing costs to products. He writes:

> Common costs and joint costs are sometimes confused, but they have an important difference: common costs can be traced to the separate products on a cause-and-effect basis or by tracing the use of facilities; they do not include direct materials and labor, whereas joint costs cannot be so traced and do include prime costs.[2]

Hence we shall conclude that the calculation of costs is the function of the accountant rather than the economist, even if we hold the question of joint costs in abeyance. Accordingly, we shall now develop accounting cost concepts within the theoretical framework that we have developed, oriented particularly toward the international oil industry, and as such concepts are generally applied in present practice.

6.1. Production Cost and Its Elements

Production cost accounting is concerned with costing methods chiefly related to manufacturing, transformation, or extraction of materials or products. Hence it is not generally interested in the distribution of goods or in services. Knowledge of production costs is useful in the determination of costs of crude oil sales and costs of inventories and this would lead to the determination of "production profits". If cost accounting could be defined as a process of classification and compilation of data included in accounting and cost records according to the purpose for which these classifications are used, costs could be divided according to their direct or indirect relation

---

1. Lawrence L. Vance, *Theory and Technique of Cost Accounting* (Brooklyn: The Foundation Press, 1952) p. 367.
2. *Ibid.*

to production units or operations. They would be fixed or variable in accordance with their relation to the volume of production. Furthermore, it is possible to obtain figures representing separate costs of production, refining, and marketing. Then the costs in each production unit could be classified according to the costs of materials and direct labor costs in addition to the other indirect expenses.

All this applies in principle to the oil industry. The methods used in the determination of the costs of the elements and portions constituting the production cost of a barrel of oil are considered relevant to the determination of net income. Furthermore, in order to facilitate the portrayal of the cost calculation picture, a clarification of some relevant characteristics of the oil industry seems to be in order.

6.1. A. International Petroleum Industry Characteristics

Related to Production Costs

Extractive industries in general are different from other industries, and the petroleum industry in particular commands some special characteristics that have bearing on the cost of production. They are:

1. *Integration* in the oil industry covers exploration for oil, development of hydrocarbon fields and producing oil and gas to the well-head, and the transportation of them, through pipelines to gas oil separation plants and stabilizers. These phases constitute what we call the process of crude oil production. Of course, full integration would add refining, transportation, marketing, and distribution, the costs of which are excluded from production costs.

2. *Large expenses* are incurred for exploration areas that finally prove unproductive.

3. The main assets of the oil industry are the *hydrocarbon deposits*, which are distinguished as assets depletable by production and, to a great extent, irreplaceable through normal industrial and technical operations. These inherent characteristics differentiate depletion from depreciation, due to the fact that the transformation process

in depletable assets is direct, while in the transformation of fixed assets into finished products it is indirect. On the other hand, duration of time has little effect on the intrinsic value of oil and gas, as opposed to fixed assets such as machines and equipment.

4. Virtually all oil and gas operations are governed by *agreements* held between the producer and the landowner; such is the case in most petroleum exporting countries where foreign owned oil producing companies are bound by agreements which govern the relation between the producing companies and the governments that have sovereignty over the concession areas.

5. The presence of *impurities* in oil also affects its cost of production.

6. Crude oil production costs are also affected by the fact that in most cases *oil is produced together with gas*, and little has been done to establish more rational and objective methods for the allocation of costs between the two. Normally, all costs are assigned to oil and the value of the gas sold is deducted from them.

7. *The location of oil fields* affects the costs of transportation to export terminals or refineries.

6.1.B. Production Cost per Barrel

Crude oil production, then, requires the locating of hydrocarbon deposits and the development of the fields for production. Exploration operations require obtaining legal permission which gives the developer the right to explore and carry out the necessary operations. Hence crude oil production costs can be classified according to pre-production costs and production costs.

6.1.C. Pre-production Costs

The cost incurred before actual production begins includes the following main items:

1. Costs of obtaining concessions.

The costs of obtaining a concession to explore for oil and gas include all expenses paid by an oil company for obtaining the concession and for the rents and other payments made afterward according to the terms of the concession agreement. These incurred expenses would maintain implementation of the agreement. Thus, they might be generally considered as naturally incurred for buying and maintaining the concession. The general case is that most of these expenses are capitalized, because their benefits extend to the end of the concession and are not confined to a specific limited financial period. Yet, some companies consider them as revenue expenses, deductible in the year of incurrence and based on the fact usually only a small part of the concession area that is productive. Hence the expenses incurred on unpromising areas are considered a loss to be deducted from the income of the year of operation. Because the expenses related to the promising areas are generally minor according to this allocation, they are similarly treated.

2. Costs of exploration.
    Exploration costs are mainly incurred for the geophysical and geological surveys which oil companies undertake to determine the presence of petroleum in concession areas. For the purpose of this study all the costs incurred in a certain field or fields, before discovery of oil, are considered as a part of exploration costs. Many petroleum companies consider this type of costs as revenue expenses, even if oil was discovered in commercial quantities. Of course, a large portion of these incurred costs do not lead to the discovery of hydrocarbon deposits in commercial quantities. The conventional procedure followed is the deduction of such expenses through depreciation in order to determine annual net income. On the other hand, some oil companies deduct these expenses from gross profits in the year of incurrence. This relates mainly to exploration in new areas whose petroleum potential has not been determined. However, there is another type of costs which deals with exploration costs incurred in producing areas, such as expenses of studies and technical research which help to determine further the field's characteristics.

3. Costs of drilling and field development.
    In the second phase of the production process the venture normally incurs the costs of drilling and development of the field. This is to prepare the field for actual production. Such costs are normally classified

as tangible expenses, as in equipment and structures which might have a salvage value, while the other expenses of labor and transportation have no salvage value.

4. Costs of gas injection and conservation of oil reserves.

   In recent years some petroleum companies incurred large expenses in technical research devoted to the conservation of oil reservoirs and increase of recoverable oil, expenses which might result in reduction of future production costs. They increase the productive capacity of the enterprise in the long run.

5. Costs of dry holes.

   The drilling of some dry wells is encountered in exploration and field development operations. Many petroleum companies tend to charge the expenses of such drilling operations to income in spite of the differences in the nature of the two types of drilling operations.

6.1.D. Production Costs

Those costs which are related to the actual production phase include the following items:

1. Direct operating expenses.

   A large portion of these expenses is divided according to the different phases of production such as lifting, gathering, separation, stabilization, transportation of the petroleum products to export terminal and refineries.

2. Indirect expenses.

   Most petroleum companies deduct these revenue expenses from gross income without allocating them in some way or another to determine the share of each produced barrel.

This summary of production costs elements indicates the general lines of such costs which are classified in stages up to the actual production of a barrel of oil.

6.2. The Accounting Net Income Formula

If we refer to net income by the letter Y and revenues by R and costs by C, we find that $Y = R - C$. The method of determining R and C is one of the most important functions of financial and cost accounting. We have seen in the previous section elements that enter C. Accordingly, net income determination for the accountant is essentially a very simple process. It is only a matter of deducting total periodic costs from total periodic revenues. At least this is what accountants usually do. The economist might not agree. His definition is quite different. Sidney Alexander says that "a year's income is, fundamentally, the amount of wealth that a person, real or corporate, can dispose of over the course of the year and remain as well off at the end of the year as at the beginning."[1] At the present time well-being is not a subject for accounting, although it is an important consideration for business judgment. However, "the economist's concept of income is designed primarily to fit the case where the future is known with certainty".[2] In the meantime the accountant must deal with recorded events in an objective manner, and this is where accounting departs from economics in income measurement.

Although a recorded event is the starting point for accounting income determination, we find that what happens behind a recorded event is also most important for the accountant. To determine what and how much to record is not always a simple question. Then our immediate problem here is what constitutes R and what constitutes C.

Revenues, R, are generally determined through quantities sold and prices obtained. Measurement of these quantities is easily achieved but prices are not always easy to see objectively, especially in the international petroleum industry.

6.2.A. Prices, Discounts, and Marketing Allowances

Petroleum is sold in the international market at prices that are related to the posted price in the exporting country. Such posted prices are generally determined by buyers rather than sellers. Yet, sales are not necessarily made at these prices. Discounts are often given. All these problems are normal in trade. However, for an international petroleum organization they

---

1. American Association of Accountants, *Five Monographs on Business Income*, The Study Group on Business Income, 1950, p. 1.
2. *Ibid.*, p. 2.

present a real problem for the accountant. Buyers and sellers are, in most cases, the same people under different names. Normally, the oil producing company is a subsidiary wholly owned by one or more of the international majors who are the buyers of its production. An arm's-length transaction is not always present. Consolidated statements are the best reflection of the whole situation, but income statements for a producing company are absolute necessities. So a price has to be agreed upon by the producing company and those parties who have interest in its earnings. Posted prices with no discounts to affiliates and with nominal marketing allowances are the generally accepted patterns in the Middle East. Other areas operate on realized prices. However, even posted prices themselves are challenged by OPEC. Reasons for such challenges are many. They are a complex mixture of economic, legal, and accounting analogies which constitute a vast area of special considerations in petroleum economics. The accountant's interest is to know the facts as they are; to know the arm's-length price, discounts, and marketing allowances. Otherwise, his income statement is weak. He should refer to these facts and make them well known.

To determine what is an arm's-length deal is really a problem of determining accounting revenue.

6.2.B Petroleum Production Cost and Income

Taking revenues as given we shall deal only with total periodic costs. We have seen that the costs of petroleum production and pre-production, added together, represent the total costs, C, in our net income formula. In this sense, C is affected by at least three factors. Nevertheless, no matter how costs are determined, whether by capitalization, amortization, depreciation, depletion, or by expensing in the year of incurrence, C always substantially represents joint costs identified with both oil and gas. If C is generally joint, as the case in the petroleum industry, and if it concerns more products than those that were identified with the income statement of any single period, it is clear that C is overstated, which results in an understatement of Y. Accordingly, we find that C can be understated or overstated, either because of indirect capitalization, depletion, depreciation, amortization, expensing policies (accounting decisions) or because of disregarding the allocation of joint costs. For convenience, we shall refer to this whole complex problem as a problem of joint costs and it will be dealt with in Chapters IX through XI.

CHAPTER VII

Prices and the Determination of Revenues

It is evident that revenues represent an essential link in income determination. Their measurement is less apparent, however, particularly in the international petroleum industry. The conventional measurement technique, as a general rule, calls for a determination of quantities and sales prices. This was already referred to in Chapter VI. Such a technique, it is argued hereafter, is inadequate. It lacks the rational and objective reflection of the realities that surround sales transactions in the said industry. This calls for the inquiry as to the existence of a relatively more objective measurement means in order to arrive at the least biased revenue quantifications. The following exposition is believed to fulfill this requirement, at least in a relative comparative manner. We shall use conventional accounting theory for revenue recognition and measurement as a first lead in the analysis of oil revenues.

7.1. Revenue Measurement

In our investigation of the external environment of our organization model, we found that accounting decisions related to the measurement of revenues are critical to the survival of the organization. This is particularly true in the case of the effect of exporting governments. An objective and unbiased formula of revenue measurement should greatly facilitate the solving of this controversy and hence contribute favorably to the survival of the organization. In the following pages an approach to this formula is sought, leaving the complexities of practical application of the chosen technique to Chapter XIII.

7.2. Transfer Prices and Revenue Determination

Concerning the definition and tests of revenue, the Committee on Accounting Concepts and Standards of the American Accounting Association writes:

> Revenues, the principal source of realized net income, are the monetary expression of the aggregate of products or services transferred by an enterprise to its customers during a period of time. In accounting for revenue, the two central questions are the timing of revenue recognition and the determination of amount.[1]

What concerns us here is not the timing of revenue recognition but the determination of its amount. Paton and Littleton put the passing of title as the essence of the completed sale, at least from the legal point of view. Moreover, they recognize that the title passing is "a highly technical matter".[2] It does, no doubt, possess such a characteristic, but passage of title is not adequate in an affiliated group. Moonitz observes that:

> Revenues and expense, for example, now refer to the affiliated group as a unit; therefore, when it is stated that revenues are, in the main, to be recognized on a sales basis, the reference is to the revenue of the group and the sales of the group. A sale does not occur, then, until a valid contract has been concluded with legal persons outside the affiliation. Mere transfers between units of the consolidated area are considered incapable of establishing gain or loss.[3]

Accordingly, transfer prices similar to the posted prices within an international petroleum organization are incapable of establishing gain or loss since no sales contract has been concluded with persons outside the organization. That is to say until a barrel of oil is sold to a consumer outside the organization, revenue to the organization as a whole, including the producing company, is indeterminate: so also is the calculation of pre-tax net income, and thus the income tax itself. We may conclude that from an accounting point of view only consolidated revenue has any

---

1. American Accounting Association, *Accounting and Reporting Standards ...*, *op. cit.*
2. Paton and Littleton, *op. cit.*, p. 54.
3. Moonitz, *The Entity Theory ...*, *op. cit.*, p. 69.

significant meaning. Yet, integration is called for, specifically integration of the producing companies with their parents to accommodate other "downstream" operations. In the same manner, the international petroleum organization could account for all its operations in a consolidated manner, with expenses, assets, and revenues properly defined.

It is highly improbable that the major international oil companies will ever agree to report income on an integrated basis identified solely with one oil producing subsidiary in any one single oil exporting country. Integration of the type required for the more objective revenue determination has long been called for, particularly by some oil exporting governments. It never appealed to the majors because of the practical and legal difficulties of prorating income among several stages of oil activities taking place in many different countries. Many oil men in the industry believe that it is virtually impossible to do anything of that sort, to the extent that they are willing to fight it in court. The fact that none of the major international oil companies report income on an integrated basis except to their home governments, is taken to be sufficient evidence of the inacceptability of the integration proposition.

Should such integrated revenues be available and identified with a single oil producing subsidiary in an objectively verifiable manner, they would definitely constitute the more objective basis for determining revenues attributable to the oil production phase only. It should be observed, however, that this procedure is correct only on the assumption that the ultimate and final sale of whatever products or derivatives is made to independent buyers outside the affiliation in a competitive market. Such products and derivatives must then be used outside the affiliation free of any tie with the affiliation on a market competitive enough to assure the independence of its ultimate buyer or buyers. Otherwise, revenues based upon such exchange prices would not reflect arm's-length dealings in the sense of "bargaining between two (or more) independent entities or evidence that is the equivalent of this standard".[1] Hence a competitively determined price is the primary lead that satisfies this criterion of independence so basic to the objective determination of revenues. Should the market for intermediate crude materials or final finished products and derivatives have substantial monopolistic tendencies, evidence to an equivalent approach to the determination of a competitive price is searched for.

Nevertheless, the integration basis of revenue determination, even

---

1. Moonitz, *The Basic Postulates ...*, *op. cit.*, p. 29.

with the assumption of the existence of arm's-length dealings for finished products and derivatives with independent parties outside the affiliation, is simply not available. In other words, since such an integrated basis seems to interfere tremendously with the practical and economic organization of the industry, through the requirement to objectively identify revenues to any one single producing subsidiary, such integrated basis is ruled out. This elimination might look arbitrary, but the virtual impossibility of applying it in practice disqualifies it for consideration, particularly with reference to the basic framework established in Chapter II. Furthermore, neither the finished product market nor the market for crude oil is yet established to be sufficiently competitive for our purposes.

This calls for the examination of the petroleum market economics as a preliminary step toward the establishment of the equivalence of an arm's-length price. Should a competitive price exist for petroleum entering into international trade and identified with the production stage, the case under consideration would be resolved. Otherwise, for practical reasons and still within the requirement of our basic choice criteria referred to above, an approximation of such a price or its equivalent must be searched for. Conventional accounting revenue measurement techniques do not seem to be capable of providing such an approximation. In fact, it has already been demonstrated in the first part of this chapter that the independence arm's-length test has to come from the market, where economics is the proper and logical tool. Hence the examination of international petroleum market economics and the utilization of the price determination tools of economic theory are called for.

7.3. Petroleum Market Economics

What an affiliated buyer would or should pay for a barrel of oil in the international trade is still an unresolved question. It is the problem of establishing a rational price structure on which the OPEC board of governors is directed "to prepare a comprehensive study", according to resolution IV. 32. The oil companies are not very eager to do so; and, in some cases they are legally prevented from defining one. They are already accused of implicit collusion and administered prices. The Shell paper referred to in Chapter I states that "an outstanding feature in this confused price situation is the fact that competing marketing companies maintain their retail prices at a stable level for a period of time, and then they all suddenly change their prices by the same amount overnight as if by design".[1]

Regarding the structure of oil prices, OPEC takes the position that any rational price structure must take into account the following considerations:

1. The demand for crude oil at the source is virtually insensitive to price changes and the price of crude oil should therefore be free from severe fluctuations. Such fluctuations would entail serious consequences in the long run for producing and consuming nations.

2. Prices should bear a reasonably close relationship to prices existing today, because any violent change over a short period of time would precipitate either too great a drop in the revenue of producing countries or too sharp an increase in the energy costs of the consuming nations.

3. Prices should, within reasonable limits, be predictable because predictability within these limits and over a period of a few years would confer on the producing nations the benefit of being able to plan their economic development with a greater measure of certainty and would confer on consuming nations the benefits of the additional security to be derived from the knowledge that prices would not fluctuate erratically.

4. Prices should take into account, and in some manner compensate for, the continually increasing prices of manufactured goods; because it is only in this way that the petroleum exporting nations, which share in common with other exports of primary commodities the problem of a trend towards deteriorating prices, can achieve the long term stability required for their economic development.[2]

OPEC's position depends essentially on the assumption that demand for oil

---

1. Wayne A. Leeman, *The Price of Middle East Oil* (Ithaca, N.Y.: Cornell University Press, 1962), pp. 57–62.
2. "The price of crude oil, a rational approach", presented by OPEC Beirut, November 5–12, 1962, IV Arab Petroleum Congress, pp. 8–9.

is inelastic and "insensitive to price changes". Hence it should not be subject to violent changes. This assumption is essentially correct in short term considerations. Middle East and Venezuela oil prices have been reduced twice since January 1959; in February 1959; and again in August 1960.[1] Yet, the production increase in 1961 was only 7.6% more than 1960, little different from the average free world increase of 5.9%. The share of Middle East oil in the world markets increased from 29.7% to 30.2%, a very small increase indeed. This is due to the fact that the demand for oil production is dependent on the capacity of the users, which normally does not expand rapidly. Nevertheless, the demand in the long run would expand, if crude oil prices should be kept consistently lower than those of other energy sources. The rest of the OPEC considerations are mainly political and do not substantially affect our conclusions with regard to the examination of prices. Oil economists have emphasized the fact that the market for international oil is a natural oligopoly.[2] Leeman, in his explanation of the market structure of Middle East Oil, states that "a few sellers form an oligopoly and almost certainly tend to behave as oligopolists, hesitating to lower prices in the expectation that reductions will be matched, reluctant to raise them for fear that rivals will not follow, yet inclining over the long run to move toward relatively high prices and 'comfortable' profit margins".[3]

Another major consideration in the world oil market structure is the fact that most of those few controlling companies own assets in both low-cost and high-cost oil producing areas. They sell oil from both types of areas but at different prices which do not depend on the geographical factors in the transportation. Thus low-cost Middle East oil can be landed in Venezuela, a higher cost major oil producer, at prices approaching Venezuelan export prices, despite the large amount of freight charges involved. Traditionally there has been, and there still is, an equalization point between Western Hemisphere (U.S. and Venezuela) and the Middle East oil, which further complicates the world oil market structure.

For example, if we take New York as a center market, we find that Middle East 36–36.9 degree crude could be landed in New York at some 18 cents

---

1. The net reductions in Middle East 34° API gravity crude, were 26 cents per barrel between January 1959 and August 1960. The U.S. Gulf Coast price of $ 3.28 for similar gravity crude has not changed since 1959. Venezuelan crude of 36° API gravity was reduced 21 cents in 1959 and 4 cents in 1960, a total reduction of about 25 cents. See Charles Issawi and Mohammed Yeganeh, *The Economics of Middle Eastern Oil*, Faber and Faber, London, 1962, p. 89.
2. Leeman, *op. cit.*, p. 245. See also pp. 57–62.
3. *Ibid.*, pp. 195–6.

lower in price than crude of similar gravity imported from Venezuela. Such difference is 44 cents if London is taken as a center of the market.

Taking Venezuela as the marginal producer in this illustration, we find that F.O.B. price of 36–36.9 degree crude is $ 2.82 per barrel, and transportation to New York at 31 cents per barrel and at 52 cents to London makes the price in those centers $ 3.13 and $ 3.34, respectively. Pricing Middle East crude of similar gravity at the same prices in these two centers and deducting transportation costs from the Persian Gulf to New York of $ 1.11 per barrel and of 92 cents to London leads to an F.O.B. price of $2.02 for crude shipped to England. These prices, compared with F.O.B. Persian Gulf postings of $ 1.84 for similar crude, find a difference of 18 cents per barrel in the case of crude shipped to the United States and 58 cents in the other case. Given the quantity of oil marketed in each area, revenues should be adjusted upward, in this instance, to reflect a more accurate picture of the situation. This sketch of the world oil market and crude oil prices is designed as a basis from which to seek a method for a rational and objective determination of revenues, since world market conditions do not permit the use of the traditional revenue accounting measurement test.

In a market of this nature, it is questionable whether the price mechanism referred to in the Shell paper can function properly without some agreement between the parties concerned on the factors affecting the determination of revenues. So far, neither economics nor accounting has been able to devise an objective formula for this type of revenue determination. They have indicated partial agreement around an equalization point, involving market sharing and base prices in major export areas. This means equality of the delivered price at a certain point between Eastern and Western producers. Such a price structure could be devised, but it would require a formula agreement between the oil companies concerned and the exporting governments dealing with them. This, in effect, is an approximation of the arm's-length test as far as its acceptability by the parties is concerned. However, since such a procedure is not yet accepted by the participants in international petroleum transactions, the problem of indeterminate revenue still exists.

We may conclude, then, that the market for petroleum entering into international trade and identified with the production stage is not sufficiently competitive for the determination of an arm's-length price. In fact, there is some evidence as to its oligopolistic nature. Hence the utilization of the other price determination tools of economic theory is proper, at least for an approximation of an equivalent arm's-length price.

7.4. *Approximating an Arm's-Length Price*

It is well known in economic theory that, under conditions of competition, inefficient high-cost producers can survive at a price equal to the total unit cost of the most inefficient producer. Such a price permits the low cost efficient producers to realize abnormal profits. Hence, in any one market, all producers sell at the same price; some barely recover their costs and a normal rate of return while others get more advantages from the situation.

Let us assume for illustration that in a defined freely competitive market there exist n number of suppliers in a certain period of time. The equilibrium price determined through the forces of demand and supply in this market is assumed to be Y, for a total supply of X_1 (see Fig. 7.1).

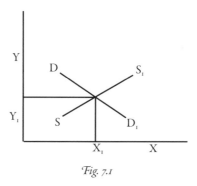

Fig. 7.1

Our approach, then, is to apply this admittedly hypothetical illustration to the international petroleum industry and derive conclusions, of which limitations will be stated later on, as a step toward the approximation of an arm's-length price.

The international petroleum market is then looked at, as a complex system composed of an m number of simple markets to be referred to as m_i. Further, an s number of petroleum suppliers exist in the complex market, m. But in any small market, m_i. it is not necessary that a total of s suppliers exist; it could be less but not more.

In this market, m_i, the prices at which suppliers consummate their sales are not uniform. This lack of uniformity is due to the lack of free competition, since most sales are made within affiliated groups. Any one affiliated group in this market, m_i buys at a different delivered (CIF) price from a subsidiary supplier in country A, compared to another in country B. Exactly the same prices are used within the other affiliated groups in the same market, m_i. In other words, there exists a number of separate affiliated groups or buyers in the market, m_i, who pay the same price for the same commodity when buying from country A and pay a different price for the same commodity when they buy from country B.

To put it differently, a realistic, rather than a purely legal or theoretical, reflection of the conditions in market m_i, would indicate that at least two suppliers simultaneously charge two different prices for the same commodity at the same market. Compare Venezuela and the Middle East. Then, if we accept the assumption that the real suppliers in market m_i, are the two countries, A and B, in which oil is produced, rather than the production subsidiaries within the affiliated groups, we find that those buyers are contradicting the simulation of a competitive market introduced hereinabove.

In a competitive market and under conditions of market equilibrium, only one price prevails. Hence if country A or the first supplier, S_1, is able to sell at a unit price, Y_1, there is no reason for the second supplier, S_2, to sell at any price below Y_1, unless he wants to drive the first supplier from the market. This is particularly true if S_1 cannot survive at a lower price because of his inefficiency.

Given the assumption that this is not the case, the second supplier would then adjust his price to make it Y_1, if simulation of competitive conditions takes place.

Referring back to our simplified illustration, we shall assume that in any given market n numbers of suppliers, i.e. countries, exist. Furthermore, we shall assume that the highest prevailing price in that market is the uniform price at which suppliers should consummate their sales. It is an approximate guide of a price that prevails under competitive conditions. As such and within the boundaries of the above stated assumptions, revenues are adjusted in a manner that reflects the existence of a higher price than the one used for determining revenues arising in a given market.

Our application of this approach of revenue measurement for a conceptual business organization belonging to the international petroleum industry leads to more than one price in any one crude export center, depending on the market of destination. The detailed practical illustration of this technique is left for Chapter XIII.

7.4. A. Inherent Shortcomings

It is evident that, since we have used several assumptions and simplifications, a word of warning seems to be in order.

We have undercut the significance of sales to independent buyers at prices far below published prices. The basic reason for not considering sales to independent buyers as representative of market conditions is the relatively small percentage of independent sales when compared with affiliated sales. This would be clear after reading Chapter XIII, which substantiates, in a tentative and relatively hypothetical manner, the writer's judgment. Nevertheless, the fact still remains that such independent sales do exist. The assessment of their significance in providing a lead toward an arm's-length test of revenues is a matter of judgment. Probably, only few would make the same assessment.

Another debatable link in the simulation of a competitive market is the assumption that the petroleum exporting countries and not the integrated oil companies are the effective suppliers in the international oil market. Legally, this is not true. Analytically, the case is different. Here, also, there are elements of judgment to which others might object. Nevertheless, we are looking to the problem with the objective of survival of the industry in mind. The oil exporting countries are an important factor in this respect. Whether they want or will become the effective suppliers should not be inferred from this assumption. It is the writer's belief, however, that survival could be promoted through reason and common sense more than through law or politics. This is, at least, one reasonable approach.

Furthermore, in the original illustration of a competitive situation, the equilibrium price is determined by market forces. Prices in the international oil industry are administered whether they are low or high. To use the high price as indicative of a competitive equilibrium price is a necessity of simulation. Should a really competitive equilibrium price exist, the whole problem disappears. The fact, however, is that the problem exists and is creating friction between the industry and OPEC. A practical solution is needed. This is only a limited attempt at one.

Finally, the question of defining the simple markets arises. Fortunately, here we are on more solid ground. We can safely define such a market as one where none of its suppliers can be spared, if its total needs are to be met. This means that the high price supplier, for economic or other reasons, can persist in the long run without the necessity of a price reduction to match other low price suppliers. Venezuelan oil in certain parts of Europe is only an example.

Hence, our conclusion that the lower price supplier must adjust his revenues to match the high price supplier makes sense.

CHAPTER VIII

The Problem of Joint Costs in the Production of Hydrocarbons

SO FAR WE HAVE BEEN mainly concerned with the conceptual and theoretical premises, related either to the entity or to its accounting activities. We have also presented, in Chapter VI, an outline of present accounting methods for income determination and proceeded to the investigation of alternative revenue measurement techniques in Chapter VII. It is time now to examine the cost-expense side of the basic accounting income formula. The joint cost problem occupies an important position in the determination of inventory book values and the cost of goods sold, as does the question of expensing or capitalizing expenditures incurred in the process of exploring for hydrocarbons. One way or the other, the treatment affects total cost of production, even with no allocation between liquid and gaseous hydrocarbons. A significant portion of this total cost, however, relates to both crude oil and natural gas and therefore is joint cost. An allocation between oil and gas is then needed if an objective reflection of what takes place in the cost stream is to be achieved. Unless such allocation is made objectively, the book cost of inventories and the cost of goods sold will be out of order. Income determination will also be so characterized.

In summation, the total joint part of the cost of producing oil and gas and that of the goods sold depends on expensing and capitalization practices. This necessitates an examination of such practices before investigating the joint cost problem in more detail. This will follow an orientation with the entire question. In Chapter IX, an examination of the current methods of joint cost allocation in the oil industry is made as a first step toward delineating the chosen alternative, which delineation will be the subject of

Chapter X. The book cost of inventories and the cost of goods sold are at least partially dependent upon capitalization-expensing practices and joint cost allocation. Their examination is delayed to Chapter XI, followed by the examination of the cost-expense side of the conventional accounting income formula. Chapter XII outlines the outcome of the study in the form of an accounting theory for the determination of a neutral value of net income.

8.1. A General Orientation

Exploration for petroleum and the development of its fields are two important stages that normally precede its production. An understanding of the activities of these three stages is a logical prerequisite to the understanding of the accounting problems identified with them. However, a detailed description of such activities is available in the accounting literature and in petroleum production economics, so we present only an outline of such activities in section 8.1.A below. The second part of the general orientation question concerns certain views as to the significance of the joint cost allocations problem and is the subject of section 8.1.B.

8.1. A. Petroleum Production

Exploring for more sources of petroleum is, in general, a definite requirement for maintaining an ever-increasing rate of production. The Petroleum Department of the Chase Manhattan Bank has undertaken a continuous study of United States and Free World oil economics. With respect to the exploration of oil one of its studies reads as follows:

> The search for oil and gas is an exceedingly expensive operation –
> for the giant corporation as well as for the individual... When it is
> conducted in remote areas, the effort includes the clearing of land
> and the construction of roads and supply lines. When the search
> is on water, huge platforms, barges or islands must be built before
> drilling can commence. In foreign lands, it is usually necessary
> to provide additionally all the facilities normally supplied in
> the United States by the community ... Having spent vast sums
> of money, the would-be discoverer of petroleum is by no means
> assured of success.[1]

---

1. John G. Winger, Harold D. Hammar, Frederick G. Coqueron and John D. Emerson,

Spending these monies seems, then, to be necessary to maintain an ever-increasing production through the discovery of more and more reserves. An accounting reflection of this situation is a critical link in income determination.

Finding petroleum is only the beginning; discovered fields must be developed. Such development involves actual drilling operations and "the building of roads and structures of various types, such as camp buildings, derricks, tanks, the development and distribution of power, the laying of pipelines and installation and operation of pumps, engines, lighting and water systems."[1] Without such activities the actual production of petroleum would be impossible. Some of the petroleum production characteristics have already been referred to in Chapter VI in relation to the present methods of determining petroleum production and pre-production costs. Such production is generally derived from oil fields. Lester C. Uren uses this term "in the sense that it constitutes a separate and 'distinct pool' or 'reservoir'".[2]

Furthermore, the productive life of a field depends, among other things, upon the relationship between the production cost and the selling price. It is a special type of relationship that has a bearing on our cost allocation methods, as will be explained in Chapter X.

Interest in the unit production cost of petroleum is not recent. Uren indicates that this question "has been the subject of several surveys at various times by various government agencies"[3] in the United States. Others in various countries are interested in such determination, aside from its important effect on income, as it could formulate a basis for certain fiscal or other policies. However, this side of the story is irrelevant to income determination.

The term "hydrocarbons" is used here to mean solid, liquid, and gaseous substances belonging to this natural resources. This, in one sense, refers basically to petroleum (crude oil) and natural gas. Appendix A gives a simplified outline of petroleum chemistry relevant to our discussion; it describes such materials in some detail. However, we are concerned with only the oil and gas association.

Uren states that "natural gas is a universal accompaniment of petroleum

---

Future Growth of the World Petroleum Industry (New York: The Chase Manhattan Bank, Petroleum Department, 1961), p. 23.

1. Lester Charles Uren, *Petroleum Production Engineering, Petroleum Production Economics* (New York: McGraw-Hill, 1950), p. 5.
2. *Ibid.*, p. 19.
3. *Ibid.*, p. 27.

in nature and is usually a valuable by-product in the production of petroleum; trapped in 'gas caps' in the crests of oil reservoirs and dissolved into the oil itself, it must usually be produced as the oil is produced."

This represents an important fact in the jointness of the costs relating to the production of hydrocarbons. It should be noticed, however, that a certain part of the natural gas produced in association with petroleum is used in the production operations. Such utilization includes power generation, heating and air conditioning, and reinjection "into the producing formation to assist in production of oil or used for gas-lifting oil in wells".[1] The rest, if not marketed, is usually flared. Frequently hydrocarbons produced contain a certain element, or elements, of impurities, namely non-hydrocarbons; sulphur compounds are a typical example. The percentage of such impurities in a unit of production differs from one producing field to another. Sulphur compounds are in general susceptible to separation from the technical standpoint. The separation of natural gas takes place in gas-oil separation plants generally referred to as G.O.S.P.'s. The definition of natural gas for the purposes of this study is confined to the four light-end hydrocarbon components: methane, ethane, butane, and propane. Whatever portion of the latter two remains in liquid form dissolved with crude oil will be considered as part of that crude.

This concludes an outline summary and frame of reference for the analysis to take place in relation to the capitalization and joint cost problems to be presented hereinafter, in addition to our basic conceptual framework of Chapter II.

8.1.B. Joint Cost Allocation: a Review

We have seen that there are several different elements in the costs which enter into the production and pre-production stages of oil and gas. All these costs are related to both oil and gas, even if the purpose of the search was to find oil, for the fact remains that the outcome of the search was a certain volume of hydrocarbon gases together with a certain quantity of hydrocarbon liquids. This leads to the question of how much exploration cost is to be assigned to the liquids and how much to the gases. Why is it generally believed virtually impossible to find a logically sound method of joint cost allocation? And why is a constant and equitable basis of cost allocation not sought?

---

1. *Ibid.*, p. 31.

In a hearing before the FPC a witness testified, with regard to some economic matters connected with the regulation of gas prices, that "it was really impossible to determine the cost of gas because essentially all costs were joint and you could not identify them with either oil or gas".[1]

Economists in general maintain the same view. Professor Adelman states that "to make laborious computations purporting to divide costs is 'nonsense' on stilts, and has no more meaning than the famous example of predicting the banana crop by its correlation with expenditures on the Royal Navy".[2] On the surface this seems true, but close investigation of the problem demonstrates that the production of hydrocarbons is a special case. And, even if the case is consistent with Adelman's view, what alternative do we have. Shall we stand still and not provide interested parties with a unit cost to serve their needs? A unit cost is definitely needed in practice and an answer, even if it can be only relatively objective, is better than no answer. Accounting can provide such a conditional answer, within a context of relative objectivity.

Because natural gas is jointly produced with crude oil in an associated manner, we find that marginal analysis is not applicable in the case where "the relative proportions of the final products can be adjusted to the relative demands".[3] But these conditions do not hold in the case of jointly produced natural gas and crude oil. Nevertheless, the allocation of the joint costs is a prerequisite to the determination of the total and average costs of any jointly produced products. But, again, many accountants and economists believe it almost impossible to find a way of attaching particular costs to any of the joint products except by purely arbitrary methods.[4] In the petroleum industry it becomes even more difficult in the cases where the hydrocarbons produced contain impurities, while it is much less complex in the case of the production of pure hydrocarbons, where the ordinary weight method is relatively objective.

---

1. S. P. Porter, "Determining the cost of finding and producing gas under federal power commission regulation", *American Petroleum Institute Publication*, vol. XXXVIII (vii) (1958), p. 9.
2. Adelman, *op. cit.*, p. 25.
3. Joe. S. Bain, *The Economics of the Pacific Coast Petroleum Industry*, Part I (Berkeley and Los Angeles: The University of California Press, 1944), p. 96.
4. *Ibid.* See also Porter, *op. cit.*, p. 9.

8.2. Exploration Costs: Expensing vs. Capitalization

Preliminary exploration is either carried out by the company's own exploration staff or delegated to an outside organization. The discovery of a new oil and gas reservoir presents the technical problem of estimating its potential reserves and determining the finding cost per unit discovered. Although an additional problem arises with regard to identifying the exploration costs for a given reservoir, especially in cases where more than one reservoir has been discovered as a result of one group of exploration activities, we shall assume that these problems of identification and reserve estimation have been fundamentally solved. Then we are left only with the problem of exploration cost determination per unit. Furthermore, part of the exploration activities prove unsuccessful, which presents the question of whether these so-called "unproductive costs" should be capitalized together with other "productive exploration" costs. And further, whether both types of costs should be capitalized. In the following pages we shall attempt to offer answers consistent with our basic theoretical structure.

Smith and Brock offer the following points[1] as relevant to the problem of expensing or capitalization of exploration costs. The supporters of expensing exploration costs contend that these costs are largely fixed and should be expensed in the period in which they are incurred. Furthermore, they argue that this procedure eliminates the detailed and arbitrary work of assigning these costs to specific acreage. And finally, they contend that over a period of time with a relatively constant development program there is little difference between expensing exploration costs and capitalizing and amortizing them. In general, these arguments resemble those offered by the supporters of the "direct costing" concept. This concept is not yet wholly accepted by the accounting profession for the purpose of inventory valuation and income determination.

We find these fixed indirect costs to be a definite necessity for extracting hydrocarbons from their subsurface formations. Hence both the direct and indirect costs have a real attachment to the product and form a basic element in their total cost. Because money has been spent both directly and indirectly, and because oil and gas have been discovered, they are necessarily connected to each other to the extent that a unit finding-cost can be determined rather accurately reflecting the historical facts. Our conclusion, then, is that

---

1. C. Aubrey Smith and Horace R. Brock, *Accounting for Oil and Gas Producers* (Englewood Cliffs: Prentice-Hall, 1959).

exploration costs, including the so-called unproductive ones, should be capitalized and ultimately assigned to the hydrocarbons discovered so that they expire on a product rather than on a periodic basis. This would reflect a more realistic picture of what happened in the cost stream.

With regard to the capitalization of productive exploration costs, Smith and Brock maintain that capitalization is supported by generally accepted accounting principles. These same principles also constitute the matching concept which says that "oil revenue and its related costs of finding and producing should enter the income stream at the same time".[1]

Few support capitalization of all exploration costs. Their arguments are similar to those cited above. The principal differences are found with regard to the definition of the productive unit. Those who support partial capitalization contend that the proper productive unit is the lease, pool, or field, while the other group considers the production or exploration programs as a whole, the proper productive unit. They argue that all exploration activities are necessary for discovery of the hydrocarbon reserves, pointing out that many unfavorable results are expected as part of the overall program. If an oil company knew all the facts, exploration itself would not be necessary. However, in order to know the unproductive from the productive, field exploration must be carried out on both. Whatever was spent in the unproductive area is really a cost for the productive, since without it the productive would not have been located. It is analogous to the concept of the calculated risk paid, which is considered an element in the total cost of operations. It is a common practice of business firms to insure against fire, theft, and other similar risks anticipated in the normal course of operations. These premiums are usually considered a part of the fixed indirect cost of such operations, to be allocated to the products or services produced by the activities of the enterprise. It is virtually certain that some of the activities of any exploration program will be unsuccessful. However since such unsuccessful activities cannot be identified in advance and thereby avoided, they ought to be considered a part of the whole exploration program and their cost a part of the total cost of finding the hydrocarbon formations.

In practice it is considered rather difficult to determine the exact amount of exploration costs to be capitalized for a specific acreage, if exploration is done by the company's own staff. Accordingly, the majority of oil companies follow the practice of expensing all the cost of their own exploration staffs.

---

1. *Ibid.*

However, payments made for exploration done by an outside organization are capitalized. The reasons underlying such practices derive from the belief that most of the activities of the exploration staff cannot be related to specific acreage to the extent that allocation is required.

The inconsistency of accounting treatment given to these two types of exploration programs is obvious. The difficulty of allocating indirect costs between different fields, and products, is ever-present in cost accounting and in itself is an insufficient reason for avoiding such allocation. If we look to the whole exploration program as an integral unit, we find that the costs can be divided between the different productive fields discovered according to the relative estimated ordinary weight of the hydrocarbon contents of each field or reservoir. This is the closest objective approximation available in the present situation.

It is recognized, however, that a longer time span of exploration would create some difficulties in application, due to the indefiniteness of future activities, whether related to undiscovered petroleum or to the determination of underground reserves of hydrocarbons already discovered. Nevertheless, the theory in abstraction is logical and consistent and can be used at least as a guide to a more satisfactory practice.

8.3. Drilling and Development Costs

The costs of drilling and development are incurred after oil and gas have been discovered, in preparation of the field for actual production. They are still joint in nature, for they relate to all the discovered hydrocarbons and are usually classified into two categories: intangible drilling and development costs (IDC), and tangible equipment costs, consisting of surface and well equipment.[1]

The IDC represent those expenditures for items having no salvage value in themselves and are incurred in connection with the drilling and deepening of wells for production purposes. They are generally defined to include, specifically, labor supplies, transportation, and similar items necessary in the following cases: (a) drilling, shooting, and cleaning of wells; (b) clearing of ground, draining, roadmaking, surveying, and geological works as necessary in preparation for the drilling of wells; and (c) construction of such derricks, tanks, pipelines and other physical structures as are necessary for the drilling

---

1. *Outline of Petroleum Industry Accounting* (New York: American Petroleum Institute, 1954), p. 74.

of wells and the preparation for the production of oil and gas. Thus we see that all labor costs and other installation costs incurred in completing the well, up to and including installation of the "Christmas tree", are classified as intangible development costs. Subsequent expenses of installing equipment are classified in the tangible costs category.

In practice, accounting methods vary between capitalization and expensing of the IDC costs. Since such costs are really unexpired costs rather than periodic expenses, expensing them results in an understatement of investment and income. Amortization, depreciation, and depletion methods related to the hydrocarbon production have a direct effect on the total cost stated in the accounting income determination formula. A more objective method of stating the elements of a unit of production cost is to follow the closest approximation of the actual sequence of costs.

Accordingly, only capitalization and unit-of-production determination of unit cost elements leads to total production costs which are not greatly biased. Yet drilling failures lead us to question the method of capitalization of the costs of such unsuccessful drillings. Such failures are not foreseeable and are therefore an essential part of the production activities. Their costs, then, are really an essential element in the total cost of the end product and therefore essential to the determination of income.

8.3. A. Cost Determination

A posteriori the end product is not obtained without the exploration, drilling, development, and production activities, and therefore all expenditures incurred are necessary to obtain it. In other words, such activities must be performed in advance; otherwise the end product would not be available for further use. It is evident that the assignable cost varies according to the accounting unit chosen. The proper accounting unit in development activities is the whole reservoir, since development activities are directed to the entire quantity of hydrocarbons discovered, which constitutes a whole field. Moreover, a well, or any group of wells, is not self-contained as in the whole field. Further, using the whole field unit, the unsuccessful wells become a part of the whole development program and hence attach to the quantity of hydrocarbons produced until that equipment, for example, has to be replaced.

A petroleum organization, then, must engage in various activities before reaching the stage of actually producing hydrocarbons for the market.

Different kinds of costs are incurred in these activities in the nature of investment in this kind of venture, which has a long service potential. Some of these costs relate to all the discovered hydrocarbons and are properly classified as depletable assets. Others, like development costs, are allocated to relatively shorter periods within the whole life of the field and must normally be related to the produced hydrocarbons until the well installations are no longer useful in production. This conforms to the general concept of depletion which is defined as a process of assigning the cost of minerals, i.e. oil and gas reserves, to their production. Accordingly, exploration and development can be categorized into the following: (a) mineral property costs or acquisition costs of the hydrocarbons reserves which include lease bonuses, fee lands, and title costs in addition to exploration costs; (b) intangible drilling and development costs; and (c) tangible lease and well equipment costs.

If such categorization is followed, and if we assume that the benefits of IDC will last for the life of the field, we find that unit-of-production depletion accounting applies to the first two categories. Subsequently, if we follow the unit-of-production depletion method, the remaining undepleted cost at the end of the period is divided by the remaining estimated recoverable reserves[1] at the end of that period. This is done to determine the depletion amount for the following accounting period.

The practice of not assigning any depletion cost to gas reserves is encountered in oil accounting, although logically a part of depletable costs should attach to gas reserves. Since these costs are joint, the problem of allocation again arises. If costs are not allocated, the cost of oil produced is relatively overstated.

8.4. Operating and General Costs of Hydrocarbons Production

Following completion of the stages of exploration and development, the field is ready for production. Of course, there are also direct and indirect elements in the operating costs of such fields. The direct cost elements relate to lifting, well servicing, repairs, and depreciation of field investment while the indirect elements include taxes, insurance, and other elements of overhead. Naturally the operating costs relate only to the quantity of hydrocarbons produced and not to all of the field reserves. Nevertheless, they again raise the same problems of joint cost allocation. Furthermore,

---

1. Smith and Brock, *op. cit.*, p. 308.

there are the general and administrative expenses which frequently are considered period rather than product costs. However, if we look at the problem in the light of the pronouncements of the American Institute of Certified Public Accountants, with regard to inventory pricing, we may conclude that a major part of these administrative costs should be assigned to the hydrocarbons produced. This necessarily requires again allocation of still joint costs, especially when some of them remain in inventories, for this reflects on the net income of the period, as the general and administrative costs are "indirectly incurred in bringing an article (hydrocarbons) to its existing condition and location".[1] Unless some administrative and general expenses are incurred, no production of hydrocarbons will take place. Hence they attach indirectly to the discovered and produced hydrocarbons. This method of allocation is being followed in many countries; Canada is a good example.[2] Even in the United States some writers support such a practice. J. S. Seidman believes that inventory is priced at only part of its cost rather than at its full costs, if administrative costs are not included.[3] The opposite argument is basically built on conservatism, but what is conservative in the balance sheet may be radical in the income statement.[4] Furthermore, Seidman argues against matching administrative expenses with sales. It is incorrect to assert that incurrence of administrative expenses is the sole function of selling.

Nevertheless, there are others, such as Jonathan N. Harris, who favor simplification and direct costing.[5] This line of reasoning may be acceptable for managerial accounting, but accounting for income determination is quite different. We must match costs against revenues and both should be determined as accurately, or with as close an approximation, as possible. If costs are not assigned to production, and if joint costs are not allocated, our basic frame of reference is violated. Income and assets are distorted and the basic objective of preparing financial statements is not being served in an objective manner.

1. *Accounting Research Bulletin 43* (New York: American Institute of Certified Public Accountants, 1953), p. 28.

2. Robert E. Waller, *Oil Accounting* (Toronto: University of Toronto Press, 1957), p. 54.

3. William E. Thomas (ed.), *Readings in Coast Accounting* (Cincinnati: South Western Publishing Co., 1960). See J. S. Seidman, "Do we mistreat administrative expenses in inventory?", pp. 255–8.

4. *Ibid.*

5. Jonathan N. Harris, "The case against administrative expenses in inventory", *Journal of Accountancy*, July 1946.

8.5 Conclusions

Capitalization, then, is the chosen technique to be followed whenever the costs incurred attach to assets that do not expire in any one period. Otherwise both the income statement and the balance sheet are affected adversely. Further, overhead expenses of all kinds must be assigned either to all the reserves discovered or to the hydrocarbons produced and inventoried, depending on whether they are exploration and development costs or operating, administrative, and general expenses. Otherwise income is not being objectively determined and assets are not being rationally valued. The same consequences will follow if such joint costs are not allocated in a more objective manner.

CHAPTER IX

Joint Cost Allocation
between Crude Oil and Natural Gas

9.1 Introduction

THE SIGNIFICANCE of joint cost allocation has already been established in its relationship to the objective determination of income. Allocation to arrive at a unit cost is an important question in its own right in many circles both for domestic and international reasons. The Federal Power Commission in the United States is only one example, particularly with regard to the pricing of natural gas. A unit cost objectively determined, whether for oil or gas, is an important consideration in oil and gas conservation policies. Nevertheless, such policies and usages of an objectively determined unit cost for oil and gas are not the subject of our discussion. Reference to them is only an indication of the significance of the unit cost question in itself. It is even more significant in income determination, which is our immediate question.

In Chapter II, the basic choice system, together with our basic accounting frame of reference, sections 2.6.A and B and 2.6.F, are particularly relevant to the joint cost allocation question. The problem is handled, basically, in light of cost allocation as a reflection of physical regrouping identified with a historical cost basis. Without violating this underlying premise, characteristics of flexibility and operationality of the related technique, as such terms have been defined in Chapter II, are among out choice-criteria. Our analysis is relative; it should not be interpreted otherwise. Hence our process of choosing by elimination is applied to the current joint cost allocation methods as the first step toward the exercise of a rational choice to be made in the following chapter, Chapter X.

9.2 Current Methods

We have seen that depletion accounting is applied only to those costs which are connected with all the quantity of oil and gas in the reservoir. These costs were generally classified as acquisition costs and IDC. Both categories are the type of cost which occurs only once at the exploration and development stage and, since it never recurs with regard to a particular reservoir, it is depleted on a unit-of-production basis.

However, the assets acquired through the incurrence of tangible development costs (tangible lease and well-equipment costs) do not continue as long as the time needed for the depletion of all the oil and gas in the reservoir. Depletion accounting could be applied to this kind of asset, if we knew the total quantity of oil and gas which could be produced up to the point at which the equipment is no longer able to function in production. In practice this is quite difficult, for the life of these assets is not a function of the quantity of oil and gas produced. It is rather a function of time. Accordingly, the annual depreciation of these assets should be divided between oil and gas produced, and, since the depletable costs apply to all the gas and oil in the reservoir, depletion accounting should divide these costs between oil and gas.

Hence a method of allocating these costs is needed. Finally, we must allocate those production costs which are incurred after the previous two stages of exploration and development. However, at this stage we should be careful to notice whether all production operations are necessary for the production of both oil and gas. After determining the identifiable amount to each product, we must apply joint allocation between the oil and gas produced.

We thereby have exploration and development costs which apply to the total quantity of oil and gas in the reservoir and which are treated by depletion. But part of the development costs for which depreciation principles are applicable are not usable for the production of all the oil and gas in the reservoir and, therefore, cannot be treated by depletion. It seems that these costs should be divided into categories. The first category includes those costs which apply to all gas and oil in the reservoir, which should be added to the depletable costs, while the other should include the cost of equipment which is to be depreciated. These costs should be considered among production costs since they apply only to produced gas and oil.

We have, then, only two categories of joint costs: (1) depletable exploration and development costs which apply to all the quantities of oil and gas in the reservoir and (2) production costs. Whatever allocation method we use to determine the depletion value applied to each unit of hydrocarbons produced, we must allocate the joint production costs according to the same method. So we can determine the production costs of each unit of the hydrocarbons produced. Thus, by adding the depletion to production cost we can determine the total cost of oil produced and the total cost of gas produced separately.

A satisfactory determination of costs depends on the accuracy of the costs allocation method used. This is the basis of our analysis.

9.2.A. The Sales Realization Method

The theory behind the sales realization method of cost allocation is that the relative market value of each product to the total market value of both products reflects the relative cost of each product to their total cost. Accordingly, if the market value of the quantity of associated gas produced represents 15% of the total market value of both products, then the gas is produced at 15% of the total costs incurred in the production of oil and gas. Of course, the validity of this allocation depends on whether the market value reflects the relative cost and whether there is really a consistent and constant market value for gas or oil.

With regard to the relationship between prices and costs, accounting literature establishes costs to serve only as a floor to prices. As long as the price is higher than this floor, there is no way of telling by comparison of the prices of any two products what their costs have been without additional data. The accounting point of view reflects the empirical determination by businessmen: it is a way to avoid the difficulties inherent in applying the economic theory of price determination. Because prices or market values do not have any absolute determinate relationship to costs, the basic assumption of the sales realization method cannot be substantiated.

But does the high market value reflect a high cost and vice versa? According to economic theory, prices reflect the equilibrium of supply and demand. But, if the structure of the market is monopolistic in some sense, then relatively high prices might not reflect high cost but rather monopoly power. And the magnitude of the margin between cost and price is really a reflection of this monopoly power. This margin might not be the same for oil and gas, for, in fact, the margin cannot be known accurately unless we know exactly the cost of producing oil and gas.

It is sometimes claimed that costs are incurred to produce revenue. If this were true, costs could be allocated according to the contribution of each product to gross revenue. Although it is true that costs are incurred in the creation of products that can be sold to return revenue to the organization, it does not follow that the cost of each product is proportional to its contribution to gross revenue. It could occur that the contribution of a commodity "A" to gross revenue is 15%, but it is not necessarily 15% of the joint costs. Indeed, it could be any percentage of the joint cost. Furthermore, if we knew its cost, the need for an allocation basis would be eliminated.

According to the sales realization method, if prices increase disproportionately for each product with regard to the other, then the cost ratio for allocation becomes different and costs of each product change accordingly, in spite of the empirical fact that they did not change. We must conclude, therefore, that the sales realization method is not in line with the historical cost regrouping in the light of the physical occurrences, our basic criteria. Hence it is rejected.

9.2.B. The British Thermal Unit Method

One British thermal unit (B.T.U.) is the amount of heat required to raise one pound of water at its maximum density through one degree Fahrenheit temperature.

The thermal content of a hydrocarbon fuel depends on what hydrocarbon elements it contains. In general, there is estimated to be between five and six million B.T.U. in each barrel of oil, while generally one thousand cubic feet of natural gas (MCF) contain about one million B.T.U. Accordingly, a method followed by many oil companies is based on this fact, and this ratio (1 : 6) is used as a basis of allocating joint costs between crude oil and natural gas.

This method assumes that petroleum organizations are producing heat units rather than oil or gas. This assumption ought to be examined since many accountants and oil men claim that the B.T.U. is the most logical and objective method of costs allocation between oil and gas available; for 90%

of crude oil and 97% of natural gases are used as fuels; that is, in the form of thermal units.

Two objections might be raised against this method. The first is that the uses to which oil and gas are put is really irrelevant. Furthermore, the heat content of each product does not necessarily reflect the costs incurred in its production, for they are not a function of this factor. Rather, they are a function of the technical processes and factors of production necessary to produce these products. Now it might be said that the prices of the factors of production are a function of the demand for these factors, and that the demand for these factors, in turn, is a function of the demand for hydrocarbons. But if the demand for these hydrocarbons is a function of their heat content then we must conclude that the prices of the factors of production, and hence the costs of the hydrocarbons, are a function of their heat content. It is obvious, though, that the monopolistic and intervening methods in the pricing of hydrocarbons have a more dominating influence on the demand for oil and gas than the heat content factor.

Furthermore, the technical specifications of the hydrocarbon are a much more important factor in determining the demand for it than its heat content, since the different forms of hydrocarbons are not perfect substitutes for each other. Thus, even though the B.T.U. is a common unit for all forms of hydrocarbons, it does not substitute in use.

This invalidates the concept of the heat content affecting the prices or the costs and factors of production. Accordingly, heat content does not properly reflect costs incurred in the production of the hydrocarbons; the demand for hydrocarbons is really a function of many factors, not simply their heat content.

Moreover, if we want to measure the costs of oil and gas according to our underlying premises, we must follow the process of production and the accumulation of the costs of each product according to their sequential incurrence. It is clear that the B.T.U. method does not follow this approach. Consequently, we must conclude that the B.T.U. method is neither as objective nor as logical as its proponents believe. The heat content ratio does not reflect the costs incurred, nor is it the dominating factor in the demand for hydrocarbons.

9.2.C. The Modified B.T.U. Method

We have seen that the heat contents of the different forms of hydrocarbons are not strictly comparable because of the imperfect substitutability in their use. Because the heat content of crude oil and natural gas are not directly comparable, it is suggested alternatively that the B.T.U. method should be applied only to interchangeable hydrocarbons, such as fuel oil, and gas. Therefore the modified ratio for cost allocation is built on the concept of a theoretical value for fuel oil ex a gas oil separation plant. This is done by subtracting refining and transportation costs from the price of a barrel of fuel oil at the refinery. The current price of a barrel of crude oil, then, is divided by the theoretical value of fuel oil. This is done in order to determine a weighting factor which takes into consideration the lack of direct correspondence of crude oil and gas. The quotient obtained in this step is multiplied by the B.T.U. ratio found in the former method. The joint costs between crude oil and natural gas are then allocated according to this new ratio.[1]

Fuel oil is only one of many forms into which crude oil is converted after refining. Although the choice of fuel oil eliminates to some extent the difficulty of comparison between crude oil and gas, the fact remains that only a fraction of the crude produced with gas is refined into fuel oil. Furthermore, an objectionable element still remains, for this is a value rather than a cost method. It depends on the price of fuel and crude oil, essentially value concepts, whose relationship to costs is not always very important. This is in addition to the fact that costs do not always vary with the changes in prices which is an inevitable consequence if the modified B.T.U. method is used.

This method also assumes, incorrectly, that costs always vary in direct correspondence to changes in prices. Thus we must conclude that the modified B.T.U. method does not solve the problem of joint cost allocation while still remaining within the sphere of our choice criteria.

9.2. D. The "Benefits Received" Method

In the "benefits received" method costs are allocated between crude oil and natural gas, "on the basis of which each of the products has benefited from the costs". This is built on the concept that each product benefits differently from the costs incurred, and furthermore, some costs may benefit only one of the two products. As a result we must analyze all costs incurred in order to determine the relationship between each product and the costs incurred. For

---

1. Smith and Brock, *op. cit.*, pp. 434–6.

example, if we have an item of one hundred dollars in our joint cost list for a process that benefits oil 80% and gas 20%, then eighty dollars is assigned to oil in the joint costs, and twenty dollars is assigned to natural gas.

This method avoids the many objectionable elements inherent in the previous three methods, and it is relatively logical to say that whenever a definite part of the process or activity performed can be identified with one of the products, that the costs of the activity or process are assignable to this product. The real question, however, is whether any portion of these technical activities can be identified absolutely with one product or the other without a highly subjective judgment. If we interchange the arbitrariness in allocation with subjectivity in the identification of benefits, then our progress toward a more objective joint cost allocation method has been hampered.

Let us return to our discussion of types of costs to see which of them is susceptible to benefits identification. We can eliminate exploration costs, since it cannot be reasonably said that a definite part of exploration activity is for oil and another is for gas. Because our interest is confined to associated gas, that is, gas found jointly with oil, it is not reasonable to say that any particular development activity is more related to oil than to gas, or vice versa.

Only after gas is separated from oil can an activity be identified with one or the other of the two products. Before this point, a conclusion built on an assumption of a separate existence of any of the joint products to help identify development activities is a falsification of the problem, for it is because of the joint existence of oil and gas that the whole problem of joint costs is established. If we eliminate this empirical observation, then the whole problem is eliminated.

This leads us to the conclusion that even development activities are not susceptible to objective identification with any of the two products. Consequently this method does not dispel an arbitrary element from cost allocation in the development stages. However, in the production stage, the "benefits received" concept is satisfactory since the identification of activities can be demonstrated through purely technical information rather than simply on the assumption of the separate existence of oil or gas.

9.2.E. The Reservoir Space Method

The basis for cost allocation according to the reservoir space method is the space occupied by each product relative to the total space occupied by the two products together. The results of such a method are unstable since the volume is subject to change according to temperature and pressure. Consequently, costs will be subject to change due to completely external factors, which is wholly illogical. It may be claimed that changes in volumes in underground reserves are immaterial, but this position is an implicit contradiction of the method which holds that costs are a function of space. Volume changes can occur and, according to the system, costs should also change accordingly. If we compare two reservoirs containing equal quantities of oil and gas in terms of weight and an equal total cost figure, we find that the relative spaces occupied by oil and gas in each reservoir are different. If this method were followed, it would lead us to the demonstrably incorrect conclusion that the assignable costs are not equal.

This is not an historical cost method and it does not follow the method of sequential reporting of events common to generally accepted accounting principles.

9.2.F. The Imputed Cost Method

When we have a gas field with little or no oil, the costing problem is not as difficult as it is in the case of jointly produced oil and gas. In this case we can determine fairly accurately the cost of non-associated gas. In the imputed cost method the result obtained in the case of the non-associated gas is used to establish a ratio for allocation to be applied in the case of the jointly produced oil and gas. However, since technical and operating conditions are rarely identical in the two cases, a cost comparison is not very meaningful. In application its subjectivity is compounded by the fact that the relative costs for non-associated oil and gas are not uniform for different gas fields. This makes it possible to have different ratios for allocation without any objective procedure to determine which of the ratios is to be used.

9.2.G. The Weight Method

According to the method of allocation on the basis of molecular weight, costs are divided between the two products on the basis of their relative molecular weight. It is considered a simple and objective method, accurate in that it assumes that oil and gas are not different products but one product in different forms. Weight is then the common denominator by which the total cost is averaged among units of the same product. Atomic methods of cost allocation, to be introduced in the following chapter, are essentially variations of the weight method.

But if oil and gas are considered different products, or if gas is considered a co-product or a by-product of oil, then the weight is only a denominator like thermal potential. Nevertheless, it is not a common denominator because the products are assumed to have a semi-heterogeneous character.

Gas, however, is different from oil in form and in a multiplicity of other characteristics. There are several "kinds" of oil and several "kinds" of gas, distinct according to the composition of each. But, because all "kinds" of oil and gas are hydrocarbons, the weight method is, at this point, the most promising of all allocation methods, as far as its consistency with our underlying choice criteria is concerned. Hence it shall be our starting point in its refinement, which follows.

CHAPTER X

Joint Cost Allocation –
The Development of a More Objective Method

10.1. An Outline of Underlying Premises

OUR SURVEY of the current joint cost allocation techniques in the oil industry indicated the potentiality of the weight method for development into a more objective one. The other techniques were eliminated in our choice process according to a given system of standards for selection, a system that was described as being devoid of market value connotations and one that adheres to the historical cost principle identified to the physical regrouping of products.

A further assumption is required as a preliminary step towards the establishment of the choice characteristics of a more objective method. Our joint cost analysis is partially dependent on the plausible assumption that all hydrocarbon compounds in their crude form are substantially homogeneous. In our judgments and for accounting purposes only, this is a realistic assumption. All the hydrocarbon compounds, liquid, gaseous or solid, are composed of carbon and hydrogen in certain substantially known relationships. Should we accept the conclusion that a natural hydrocarbon substance is the commodity produced, rather than oil or gas as products and by-products, our problem would be more susceptible to a more objective solution. Section 10.3 which follows, is a technical reference to this basic assumption. It is believed that the said section constitutes sufficient substantiation of the underlying premise for the sole purpose of developing a more objective joint cost allocation method.

Leading from this assumption, our choice criteria in this respect will be established in section 10.4 afterwards.

10.2. Unit Cost and the Price of Oil and Gas

We have concluded in Chapter VII that the international petroleum market is relatively oligopolistic and that prices are not freely set; they are administered. Furthermore, the present profit margins between unit cost and export price, in the language of Wayne A. Leeman, are "comfortable". Hence it is unlikely that any conceivable change in unit cost, whether arising from joint cost allocation or otherwise, would manifest itself as a change in price. The average profit margin in the Middle East is estimated by Leeman as $.82 per barrel after taxes. Therefore, unless structural competitive changes take place in the international oil market, unit cost would remain as an insignificant factor in setting prices.

The case for gas is not quite the same. So far in many areas outside North America a significant portion of the produced gas is flared. But the picture is changing. More and more plans for the utilization of gases are announced. Demand is in a process of growth. However, whether the assigned cost would affect the setting of prices is doubtful, until the time comes where demand is in excess of the existing amount of flared gases. Should such time come, and should the prevailing price at that time be below the assigned gas unit cost, the rise in demand would probably lead to a price equal to or higher than this assigned unit cost. It depends upon the relationship between the available supply of gas and the effective demand for it, still probably in a context of a monopolistic market. This is particularly true in the case that such gas does not enter the international trade as a liquified material and is not sold to more than a few local buyers. Otherwise, a case of monopsony would exist.

Thus if cost were ever to influence the price, it would be through its role as a floor in the price setting.

10.3. One or More Products

All the cost allocation methods we have discussed have assumed that gas is a by-product of oil; some have even considered oil and gas to be two different products. This underlines the statement frequently heard that the basic purpose of an oil company is to produce oil, and that whatever revenue comes from gas is considered as a reduction in the cost of producing oil. However, this is irrelevant to our problem since we are interested in what actually occurred in the cost stream of the company rather than its managerial policies.

Oil and gas are only terms for a family of gases, liquids and solids known chemically as hydrocarbons. The main characteristic of this family of chemical compounds is that every member is composed of carbon and hydrogen atoms. The number of these atoms differs from one member of the family to the other according to known mathematical formulas explained in Appendix A. In addition to carbon and hydrogen, other elements are sometimes found, but they are not considered to be a part of the essential chemical characteristics of the hydrocarbons. Hence, they are usually referred to as impurities which do not conform to any systematic relationship. The absence of any of these impurities does not affect the properties of any member of the hydrocarbon family, except for the improvement in quality, since in their pure form hydrocarbons are composed of carbon and hydrogen only.

If we know the number of the carbon atoms in each molecule of any member of the hydrocarbon family, we can determine the number of hydrogen atoms according to one of three mathematical formulas: (1) The paraffins (C_nH_{2n+2}); (2) The naphthenes (C_nH_{2n}); and (3) The aromatics (C_nH_{2n-6}). If the hydrocarbons are in their pure form, it does not make much difference whether we express production in terms of x atoms of hydrogen, or M barrels of oil and N cubic feet of gas.

10.4. Criteria for a More Objective Selection

In our discussion of the various methods of cost allocation which could be applied in the division of joint costs between oil and gas, we found that none of these methods was satisfactory to our purposes. However, the standards against which these methods were measured were not clearly identified in a generalized manner, for the deficiencies present in one method differ fundamentally from those in other methods. Although we may dismiss any method if it contains a particular and unique deficiency, we must define the general characteristics of a satisfactory method of cost allocation before we can develop a specific one that is more objective. Such characteristics are the subject of the rest of this section.

10.4.A An Historical Cost Basis

Any method of cost allocation should be an historical one in the sense that it should report, in sequence, events in the cost stream identified with each product separately. If accounting is to be considered a rational discipline, it must rest upon systematic purposive analysis, rather than subjective and highly generalized judgment.

It should be a cost method rather than a value method. That is to say, it must present actual original costs which can be attached to the particular product or asset. This is in accordance with the cost principle, a generally accepted accounting concept. *In the Accounting Research Bulletin* Number 43, we find the following statement concerning inventory pricing:

> The primary basis of accounting for inventories is cost, which has been defined generally as the price or consideration given to acquire an asset. As applied to inventories, cost means in principle the sum of applicable expenditures and charges directly or indirectly incurred in bringing an article to its existing condition and location.

This statement should apply to any joint cost allocation method chosen for the purpose of inventory costing for income determination. In this sense, values are defined as estimates about the future, while original costs are connected with the past. Hence, values as defined here are viewed as subjective and unstable estimates, while original costs are verifiable occurrences. In accounting income determination and inventory costing, a cost method offers objectivity and stability of results, which are not found in value methods.

10.4.B. Flexibility and Operationality

The method should be *flexible and operational* in the sense of being applicable under most practical situations without leading to obscured conclusions and free of as many practical complications as possible.

10.4.C. No Allocation to Unutilized Materials

Furthermore, joint costs should not be allocated to those materials produced that have no conceivable use in enterprise operations or through sale to outsiders. This is only reasonable as long as we are concerned with income determination. There is no real purpose served by such allocation except as an exercise in arithmetic. The allocated cost in this case could be considered as a loss and charged to income accordingly. This is probably more informative no doubt. Revenues are essentially derived from utilizing produced materials either by sale or through use in enterprise operations. Further, such a "loss" is incurred only because of the necessary accompaniment of gas with oil in production. Nevertheless, in the case of an international oil company, the appearance of such a loss in their financial statements might be interpreted in a manner that may contribute unfavorably to enterprise relations with the oil exporting governments. As such it violates one of the most basic choice criteria established for selecting income determination techniques. In the case of utilized or sold substances the question is different. Assignment of all the cost to oil with no cost assigned to gas would still make a difference in the determination of the ultimate net income figure, especially where part of the joint cost is applied against reinjected gas. In this case, the applied cost is to be capitalized since it concerns oil and gas relating to future operations.

Furthermore, the assignment of a certain part of the cost to gas used in enterprise operations or sold to outsiders is more in line with favorable relations with the exporting governments.

Derivation and disclosure of oil and gas unit costs indicate a more efficient use of a depletable natural resource. Already, there are many accusations of a wasteful use of resources directed against many international oil companies in the Middle East and elsewhere. If gas is actually used for re-injection purposes or for selling the enterprise will be better off by assigning costs for such purposes. A reasonable and objective cost allocation method would serve the purpose better. Several oil companies have been looking for a method of this sort to use, other than the sales realization method or other market oriented methods which are incapable of serving the purpose of costing reinjected gas, since in frequent situations, no market does really exist.

10.4. D. Cognitively Rational Choice

The selected allocation technique must be chosen in a rational manner in the sense of being oriented towards a given purpose or a set of purposes within the above-mentioned criteria. The basic conceptual framework of Chapter II is, of course, at the top of all these considerations.

10.5 The Weight Problem

We can determine the cost of the hydrogen atom produced if we express (the weight of carbon atoms in terms of) the total weight of hydrogen atoms as (H_w) and then divide the total cost (C) by H_w. Moreover, since the carbon atom weighs twelve times as much as the hydrogen atom, the relative cost of producing a carbon atom is twelve times the cost of producing a hydrogen atom.

This is an atomic weight problem regardless of whether hydrogen or carbon is weighed. One type of atom is expressed in terms of the weight of the other type of atoms. Hence, since the carbon atom is twelve times as heavy as the hydrogen atom, the relative weight of a hydrogen atom is 1/13th of the total atomic weight of one carbon and one hydrogen atom. Thence the relative cost is 1/13th of one carbon and one hydrogen atom combined and is 1/13th of the total cost of producing the two atoms. This relationship is needed for arriving at a weighted average of the apportioned costs to be developed later in this chapter as the mixed hydrocarbon atom method.

Now if cost C is divided among the hydrocarbon members produced according to the H_{wi} (the weight of the hydrogen atoms) in each of them relative to the H_w. the result is equivalent to the one obtained by dividing C according to the total weight, for the percentage weight of each member relative to the total weight of the hydrocarbons produced is equivalent to the percentage of H_{wi} of that member in relation to the H_w of all members.

10.5. A Refinement of the Weight Method

Suppose we have three hydrocarbon members *a*, *b* and *c* where their weights are *x*, *y* and *z* and their atomic weights expressed in terms of the weight of a hydrogen atom, are x_1, y_1, *and* z_1. In the case of the absence of impurities, cost divided according to the weights *x*, *y*, and *z* relative to the total weight is equal to the cost divided according to x_1, y_1, *and* z_1, relative to the total weight. On the surface of it, there is no purpose served by atomic weights. We can use pounds, tons or any other weight measurement unit as well. However, two reasons motivate a further refinement. The first one is that carbon and hydrogen atoms are *not distributed evenly* among the members of the hydrocarbon family. For two identical weights of two different members, one would possess more carbon and less hydrogen in terms of weight than the other. In other words, the first may be more heavily weighted by carbon than the other for two reasons. First, it contains more carbon atoms than the other and secondly the carbon atom is twelve times as heavy as the hydrogen atom. Hence, any cost allocation according to weight alone with no modification would be inclined towards members *possessing more carbon than hydrogen*. It is a relative distortion inconsistent with a realistic identification of regrouped costs with the regrouped physical picture. The latter indicates the production of hydrogen as well as carbon though in a chemical compound form. Why should we favor one over the other, if we can, even partially, reduce such a distortion. To put it differently, we are jointly producing carbon and hydrogen. Hydrogen and carbon do exist by themselves in pure form. In our case they are chemically united although they can technically be separated. Nevertheless, this is beside the point. What concerns us is the joint production of hydrogen and carbon in a chemical form called hydrocarbon or gas and oil. The existence of these two elements in the produced compound should be recognized, if we desire to reflect a more objectively realistic picture of an existing situation. Hence, their relative atomic and molecular structure should be recognized in our cost allocation. It can be partially taken care of through using their atomic structure and relationship as a weighting factor to be applied to their relative weights in one or more members of the hydrocarbons produced. It would be more so, if we use molecular weights instead. This will reasonably approximate an identification of costs with their physical counterparts. This takes us as deep and as close to the basic composition of the substance as is feasible and practical under the circumstances. This is one of the main and basic reasons for taking the trouble to establish the refinement of the weight method to be introduced throughout the rest of this chapter.

The other motivation underlying the movement towards the refinement of the weight method lies in the virtual existence of impurities in the produced hydrocarbons. It is a fact that must be recognized in the allocation of costs specially in the case of the utilization of such impurities for enterprise purposes or for sale to outsiders. The question, of course, is how? In the case of hydrogen and carbon a known atomic and molecular relationship exists to help in the solution. The case for impurities is not the same. They do not belong to the hydrocarbon family and generalizations about their kinds or percentages cannot be made. Such kinds and percentages differ from one oil field to the other.

Our approach is a practical one. It only allows us to move forward to the point where a practical solution, refinement or approximation of a solution seems to exist. In the case of hydrocarbons, a refinement of the weight methods seems to exist. So we approached it. In the case of impurities, a refinement of the weight method is not in sight. The only way available and consistent with our framework is to draw back to the weight method as far as impurities are concerned.

10.5.B. *Accounting for Impurities*

Within our basic characteristics established in section 10.B of this chapter, the choice of the weight method for the assignment of cost to usable impurities seems to be in order. Hence, in the case that such impurities or part of them are separated for sale or for use in enterprise operations, the total joint cost is to be allocated between hydrocarbons and impurities on a relative weight basis. Whatever cost is assigned to hydrocarbons is then further allocated according to the refined weight method introduced hereafter. Should no separation take place and hence no utilization of such impurities takes place, all the joint costs are assigned to hydrocarbons and allocated between them accordingly. The utilization of the atomic methods would partially eliminate the distortion arising from such impurities through hydrogen and carbon atom weighting process. Such a process would weight costs in favor of the carbon and hydrogen contents of the produced hydrocarbons and impurities by using the hydrogen and carbon atoms as weighting factors.

10.5.C. *Accounting for Flared Gas*

We have already established the conclusion that assigning a cost to flared gas is inconsistent with our conceptual frame of reference. Hence, for income determination purposes, no cost allocation is necessary as far as unutilized materials are concerned including flared gas.

10.5.D. *Accounting for Reinjected Natural Gas*

It is sometimes technically and economically feasible for an oil and gas producer to reinject back all or part of the associated gas produced into the subsurface formations. This procedure, in general, contributes to higher oil recoverability. In other words, it increases the productivity of the field. For example, instead of recovering 20% of the oil in place, the reinjection process may make possible the recovery of 10% or more, thus raising the field's productivity by 50% of the original recoverable oil.

In cases like this, the cost of the reinjected gas together with the reinjection costs, represent a development cost. It is the cost of developing and making available for production, oil that has been discovered. Certain technical reasons are partially overcome by gas reinjection to the extent that an extra amount of oil is producible. Hence, costs allocated to the reinjected gas in addition to the reinjection operating costs must be capitalized and depleted whenever that extra oil is produced.

10.5.E. Symbolic Formulation of the Weight Problem

In order to develop the atomic joint cost allocation techniques, the problem is symbolically stated on the basis of hydrocarbons with no impurities. This is assuming that utilizable impurities have already been assigned a cost on a weight basis. Unutilized impurities are, by definition, assigned no cost. Further, it is assumed that all hydrocarbons produced are utilized. In other words, if there are flared gases, they have been deducted from the total quantity subject to cost allocation.

$$W = w_1 + w_2 + ... + w_i + ... + w_n \qquad (1)$$

where n = the number of hydrocarbon members,
$\quad\quad\quad w$ = the total weight of the hydrocarbons produced,
$\quad\quad\quad w_i$ = the weight of hydrocarbon member number i.

The following two equations are given and accepted without proof. When H_w is converted to tons, pounds or similar weight measures,

$$H_w = W \qquad (2)$$

where H_w = the total atomic weight of carbon and hydrogen atoms in all the quantity of the hydrocarbons produced, expressed in terms of the weight of hydrogen atoms.

But:

$$H_w = H_{w1} + H_{w2} + ... + H_{wi} + ... + H_{wn}$$

and

$$W = w_1 + w_2 + ... + w_i + ... + w_n$$

Therefore

$$H_{w1} = {}_{w1}, \qquad H_{w2} = {}_{w2} \dots H_{wi} = w_i \qquad\qquad (3)$$

and $H_{wn} = w_n$; after conversion to tons, pounds or similar weight measures.

Assuming that C = the total cost of the hydrocarbons produced, then

$$C \cdot \frac{w_i}{w} = \frac{CH_{wi}}{H_w}$$

$$(4)$$

Therefore the cost of hydrocarbon member number 1 is:

$$C \cdot \frac{w_i}{w} \text{ which is equal to } \frac{CH_{wi}}{H_w}$$

10.6. The Atomic Joint Cost Allocation Methods

We have concluded that a refinement to the weight method is required to take into consideration the presence of more carbon in certain compounds than in others and less hydrogen. Moreover, the existence of impurities adds to the dissatisfaction with the said method. We also have concluded that the proposed weighting process partially minimizes such dissatisfaction. Hence, the atomic joint cost allocation methods are chosen for the purposes of the measurement of unit costs in the income determination process.

Three additional joint cost allocation methods are developed in this section for that reason. The first is based on the carbon content of the hydrocarbon compound. It is called the pure carbon atom method. The second is based on the hydrogen atom content of the hydrocarbon compound. It is called the pure hydrogen atom method. The third is a weighted average of the first two. It is called the mixed hydrocarbon atom method. These atomic methods use the relative weights of the hydrocarbon members as a starting point. Such relative weights are then weighed by the number of carbon atoms in the molecule. The relative weight of each member is weighed by the number of carbon atoms in its molecule. The weighted quantities are then transformed into percentages. These percentages are then used as a basis of allocation of joint costs between the members concerned, be they gas or liquid hydrocarbon.

The same process is repeated this time using the number of hydrogen atoms in the molecule of each member concerned as a weighting factor against its relative weight.

Finally, the percentages obtained from the pure carbon atom method are weighed by a given factor, This factor is the relative weight of the hydrogen atom in relation to the weight of the carbon atom.

10.6. A. The Basic Data

Suppose that 18 tons of hydrocarbons without impurities are produced. The chemical analysis of the hydrocarbons produced would prove the following:

Quantity excluding impurities (in tons)	Hydrocarbon member
10	Tridecane
5	Octadecane
2	Octane
1	Butane
18	

We want to determine the proportions (in percentages) of cost allocation to be used according to the normal weight and to the atomic weight methods.

10.6. B. The Normal Weight Method

Normal weight proportions are:

$$10 : 5 : 2 : 1$$

Formula: $C_{wi} = \frac{w_i}{w} \times 100.C$ (where C_{wi} = the cost of hydrocarbon member i)

The results are tabulated as follows:

Hydrocarbon member	Quantity in tons	Cost percentage
Tridecane	10	55.6
Octane	2	11.1
Octadecane	5	27.7
Butane	1	5.6
Total	18	100.0

10.6.C. The Pure Carbon Atom Method

Once we have concluded that we should "weight" the normal weights, then we must decide whether we should weight the carbon atoms or the hydrogen atoms. In the formulas of the hydrocarbons under their different classifications[1] we find that the number of carbon atoms in any one member of the hydrocarbon family does not vary under any classification, whereas the number of hydrogen atoms does vary. Consequently, the carbon atom weighting factor is more general than the hydrogen atom weighting factor, a characteristic which makes it easier and faster in application. Although it has a bias against lighter hydrocarbons, the carbon atom method more nearly satisfies our given characteristics.

The results built on basic data are tabulated as follows:

Hydrocarbon member	Carbon atoms per molecule (C_i)	Quantity in tons (W_i)	Weighted quantity (C_iW_i)	Cost percentage (K_{wi})
Tridecane	13	10	130	53.17
Octadecane	18	5	90	37.50
Octane	8	2	16	6.66
Butane	4	1	4	1.67
Total	43	$18 = W$	240	100.00

Formula:

$$K_{wi} = \frac{w_i \cdot c_i}{\sum\limits_{i}^{n} w_i \cdot c_i} \cdot 100$$

Accordingly, when the hydrocarbons of more than one member of the family are produced, costs can be determined for each petroleum product if we can determine the normal weight for each elementary compound. Then the cost of each is determined as above. If we add the costs of these members, we can determine the whole cost of the petroleum product, like crude oil or natural gas.

---

1. The American Institute of CPAs, *Accounting Research Bulletin No. 43*, p. 28 (New York, 1955). See also *Accounting and Reporting Standards for Corporate Financial Statements and Preceding Statements and Supplements*, American Accounting Association (Columbus, Ohio, 1957). On page 6 of this booklet, we find that only cost methods are mentioned for inventory pricing and the determination of the cost of goods sold. This excludes by implication any other method for pricing inventories as unacceptable to the Committee on Accounting Concepts and Standards of the American Accounting Association.

If $\mathcal{W} = w_1 + w_2 + \dots + w_i + \dots + w_n$ = the weight of the hydrocarbons; and $c_1, c_2, \dots, c_p, \dots, c_n$ represent the number of carbon atoms in each compound; and $w_1 c_1 + w_2 c_2 + \dots + w_i c_i + \dots + w_n c_n = \overset{n}{\underset{1}{\sum}} w_i c_i$; then the percentages of allocation are:

$$\frac{w_1 c \cdot 100}{\underset{1}{\overset{n}{\sum}} w_i c_i} + \frac{w_2 \cdot c_2 \cdot 100}{\underset{1}{\overset{n}{\sum}} w_i c_i} + \frac{w_i c_i \cdot 100}{\underset{1}{\overset{n}{\sum}} w_i c_i} + \frac{w_n \cdot c_n \cdot 100}{\underset{1}{\overset{n}{\sum}} w_i c_i} = 100$$

In spite of our basic premise that all the hydrocarbon members are essentially the same product, and that their dominating characteristic is the presence of carbon and hydrogen, the fact remains that each member has a different amount of carbon and hydrogen. The weighting process accounts for this difference in carbon and hydrogen contents. The pure carbon atom method chooses the carbon atom contents in the molecules of each hydrocarbon member as its weighting factor, and carbon contents are represented in the calculations since carbon is considered as the basic part of the hydrocarbon compounds.

10.6. D. The Pure Hydrogen Atom Method

The difference between the hydrogen atom method and the carbon atom method is a difference in the weighting factor. The weighting factor chosen here is the number of hydrogen atoms in the molecule of each member of the hydrocarbons family. These figures are not as general as the ones for the carbon atoms, for the number of hydrogen atoms differs according to the formulas given for the different categories of hydrocarbons. Yet, they are determinate. Nevertheless, if hydrogen is considered more basic than carbon, then the hydrogen atom content in the molecule will be chosen. This is applied to the same example discussed before; however, since a hydrocarbon member could have different number of H-atoms according to its classification, we shall restrict our illustration to paraffinic hydrocarbons only.

Hydrocarbon member		Normal weight in tons	Paraffins	
			Formula	H-atoms
Tridec	-ane	10	$C_{13}H_{28}$	28
	-ene			

Hydrocarbon member		Normal weight in tons	Paraffins	
			Formula	H-atoms
Octadec	-ane	5	$C_{18}H_{38}$	38
	-ene			
Oct	-ane	2	C_8H_{18}	18
	-ene			
But	-ane	1	C_4H_{10}	10
	-ene			
		18		

The results, then, of the application of the method could be classified in the following manner:

Formula:

$$K_{wi} = \frac{w_i \cdot h_i \cdot 100}{\sum\limits_{i}^{n} w_i \cdot h_i}$$

Hydrocarbon member		Normal weight w_i	Paraffins weighted quantity $w_i h_i$
Tridec	-ane	10	280
	-ene		
Octadec	-ane	5	190
	-ene		
Oct	-ane	2	36
	-ene		
But	-ane	1	10
	-ene		
		18	566

Hydrocarbon member		Cost percentages (Kw_i) paraffins
Tridec	-ane	54.26
	-ene	

Hydrocarbon member		Cost percentages (Kw_i) paraffins
Octadec	-ane	36.82
	-ene	
Oct	-ane	6.98
	-ene	
But	-ane	1.94
	-ene	
		100.00

If $W = w_1 + w_2 + ... + w_i + ... + w_n$ and n equals the number of hydrocarbon members produced, and W = the total weight of the hydrocarbons; and if $h_1, h_2, ..., h_i, ..., h_n$ represent the number of hydrogen atoms in each member; then $w_i h_i$ represents the weighted quantity and $\sum_i^n w_i h_i$ represents the total weighted quantity:

and the percentages of cost allocation are:

$$100 \cdot \frac{w_1 h_1}{\sum_i^n w_i h_i} + \frac{w_2 h_2}{\sum_i^n w_i h_i} \cdot 100 + ... + \frac{w_i h_i \cdot 100}{\sum_i^n w_i h_i} + ... + \frac{w_n h_n}{\sum_i^n w_i h_i} \cdot 100 = 100$$

The paraffins are taken as generally representative of the two other classifications. The pure hydrogen atom method is built on giving more importance to hydrogen in the hydrocarbon compounds. However, if hydrogen and carbon are equally essential, basic and important, the only way to represent this fact is to take a weighted average of the two methods, a procedure which is followed in the mixed hydrocarbon atom method.

10.6.E. The Mixed Hydrocarbon Atom Method

In the two previous methods, we have encountered certain biases towards either heavier or lighter hydrocarbons. Further, personal judgment must be used to decide whether carbon or hydrogen is more basic to the hydrocarbon compound. The mixed hydrocarbon method is applied to eliminate these disadvantages. This method is a combination of the previous two methods through a weighted average. Since the carbon atom weighs approximately twelve times as much as the hydrogen atom, we shall multiply each one of the cost percentages of the pure carbon atom method by twelve to make the percentages of the two methods more comparable in averaging. Then we divide by twelve and one to get a weighted average of the results. This is done as follows:

$$1/13\left(\frac{12 \cdot w_i c_i \cdot 100}{\sum w_i \cdot c_i} + \frac{w_i \cdot h_i \cdot 100}{\sum w_i \cdot h_i}\right) + 1/13\left(\frac{12 \cdot w_2 \cdot c_2 \cdot 100}{\sum w_i \cdot c_i} + \frac{w_i h_2 \cdot 100}{\sum w_i \cdot h_i}\right) + (\dots) +$$

$$1/13\left(\frac{12 \cdot w_i c_i \cdot 100}{\sum w_i \cdot c_i} + \frac{w_i \cdot h_i \cdot 100}{\sum w_i \cdot h_i}\right) + (\dots) + 1/13\left(\frac{12 \cdot w_n c_n \cdot 100}{\sum w_i \cdot c_i} + \frac{w_n \cdot h_n \cdot 100}{\sum w_i \cdot h_i}\right) = 100$$

Therefore $\qquad K_{xi} = 1/13\left(\frac{12 \cdot w_i c_i \cdot 100}{\sum w_i \cdot c_i} + \frac{w_i \cdot h_i \cdot 100}{\sum w_i \cdot h_i}\right)$

10.6.E.1. Preliminary Calculations: Paraffins:

Hydrocarbon member	Application of the formula	Cost percentages
Tridecane	$1/13\left[12(84.17) + 54.26\right]$	54.2
Octadecane	$1/13\left[12(37.50) + 36.82\right]$	37.4
Octane	$1/13\left[12(6.66) + 6.98\right]$	6.7
Butane	$1/13\left[12(1.67)\,1.94\right]$	1.7

The results of the four methods are tabulated as follows: (only paraffins are considered

The ordinary weight method	Pure carbon atom method	Pure hydrogen atom method	Mixed hydrocarbon atom method
55.56	54.17	54.26	54.18
27.78	37.50	36.82	37.45
11.11	6.66	6.98	6.68
5.55	1.67	1.94	1.69
100.00	100.00	100.00	100.00

10.7. The Evaluation of Results

Because the quantity of each hydrocarbon member relative to the total amount produced differs from one reservoir to another, and because the figures given for quantities produced put in this example are purely illustrative, we shall interpret these results according to line rather than column. The difference between one column and the other is due to the weighting factor. Although the weighting factor makes an important difference between the weight method and the atomic methods, the difference between the atomic methods is relatively immaterial. Nevertheless, there are some slight differences is results and in basic philosophy between the three atomic cost methods themselves which influence the choice of methods for joint cost allocation.

The difference in cost percentages between the weight method and the atomic methods is due to the weighting factors. The slight difference in cost percentages between carbon and hydrogen atom methods are due to the emphasis on carbon content in the first method and the emphasis on hydrogen content in the latter method. The mixed hydrocarbon atom method averages such differences out through a weighted rather than a simple averaging process. The results are more refined and less subjective.

Nevertheless, the use of relative weights as a starting point seems to lead to a double weighting process, through the consideration of carbon itself and then carbon atoms. The same conclusion applies when weighting the relative weights by hydrogen atoms. Replacing relative weights with relative molecular weights and mols partially eliminates the double weighting inherent in the purely atomic methods. Such a procedure allows us to deal only with molecules and atoms, the chemical underlying structure of the hydrocarbons substances under consideration. It leads to a more objective identification of the joint cost with the regrouped physical picture by reflecting, in financial terms, the basic chemical structure of such a picture as realistically as possible.

Furthermore, the adoption of the atomic joint cost allocation formulae to take care of mols and molecular relative weights as substitutes for tonnage or similar other weight measurements, reduces the application complexities to a minimum. It does so through the immediate availability of molecular weights through the use of published charts and tables, as well as formulae. Hence, only crude oil and whatever gases accompany it are considered in the form of two categories; i.e. oil and gas. Once the cost percentage is calculated for a certain gas/oil ratio and composition, that percentage can be used afterwards without the need for recalculation. Such a percentage is calculated as an example for one barrel of 36° API crude with a gas ratio of 500 SCF per barrel. The formulae and their application are introduced in section 10.6.A. and in Appendix B. They are identified as the carbon atom-mol method and the hydrogen atom-mol method.

10.8. Choosing a More Operational Method

So far it is demonstrated that the atomic joint cost allocation methods are more in line with our choice-criteria set out in the first part of this chapter. Only their operationality is in doubt. Furthermore, the double-weighting arising from the use of relative weights is felt to contribute to a relatively distorted outcome.

These two relatively unsatisfactory characteristics were met in the attempt to use such methods in practice and to test their consistency. In 1961, the writer, in cooperation with some engineering and accounting officials from the Arabian American Oil Company of Dhahran, Saudi Arabia, made an attempt to apply the atomic methods using empirical data relative to company operations. It was felt at that time that such methods as have been developed hereinabove were too demanding on technical information. Later on, the same feeling prevailed in other academic and business circles where the additional question of double-weighting was met. As an outcome of these academic and business contacts with the Universal Oil Products Company of Des Plaines, Illinois, the atom-mol methods have been developed in a more simplified form. This simplification is based on relatively standard data for crude oil of $36°$ API gravity. As will be clear after reading the subsequent section, similar applications can be achieved for crudes of other gravities and production conditions with different gas oil ratios and compositions.

10.8. A. The Atom-Mol Methods

The following formulae were developed in sections 10.6.C. and 10.6.D:

Pure carbon atom method

$$K_{\omega i} = \frac{w_i \cdot c_i \cdot 100}{\sum\limits_{i}^{n} w_i \cdot c_i} \tag{1}$$

Pure hydrogen atom method

$$K_{\omega i} = \frac{w_i \cdot h_i \cdot 100}{\sum\limits_{i}^{n} w_i \cdot h_i} \tag{2}$$

where $K_{\omega i}$ is the cost percentage for a hydrocarbon member *(i)* according to the allocation method used, and *wi* is the weight of the hydrocarbon member concerned,

c_i is the number of carbon atoms in one molecule of the member concerned, and

h_i is the number of hydrogen atoms in one molecule of the member concerned.

The atom-mol methods require the use of molecular weights and mols in substitution for other weight measurements – the molecular weight of a hydrocarbon member or a categorized group of members is referred to as m_i. Mols are referred to as $\mathcal{M}_i$. Hence, the formulae take the following forms:

Carbon atom-mol method

$$K_{\mathit{mi}} = \frac{\mathcal{M}_i \cdot c_i \cdot 100}{\sum\limits_{i}^{n} m_i \cdot c_i} \qquad (3)$$

Hydrogen atom-mol method

$$K_{\mathit{mi}} = \frac{\mathcal{M}_i \cdot h_i \cdot 100}{\sum\limits_{i}^{n} m_i \cdot h_i} \qquad (4)$$

The simplification is based on the immediate accessibility to the necessary information required to apply this formula. Carbon and hydrogen atoms can be calculated by the application of certain chemical formulae which are explained in Appendix A. If we take a number of hydrocarbon compounds together, the average number of carbon or hydrogen atoms in the molecule is used. An illustration is given in the example presented in the following section.

Molecular weights of gases can also be estimated according to available formulae. From the accountant's standpoint, technical calculation of this nature can always be supplied by the engineers.

Approximate molecular weights for crude oils of different gravities are also available in a relatively simple chart presented in Appendix B as Chart A1. Knowing molecular weights and pound weights, we can determine the mols.

Hence, values for the variables in the two formulae are readily available. The following example is an indication of the relative operationality and objectivity of the atom-mol methods.

10.8.B. Simplified Calculation of Percentages for Joint Cost Allocation

Technical information for the following calculations is available in Appendix B together with sources of such information. Assume:

- A. 500 SCF of gas associated with one barrel 36° API crude;
- B. Gas composition by mol. percentages are 40% methane, 25% ethane, 20% propane and 15% butane.

Then for one barrel of 36° API gravity crude and 500 SCF of gas, the following data is derived:

Hydrocarbon member	w_i quantity lb	c_i carbon atoms	h_i hydrogen atoms	m_i molecular wt..
Gas	41.8	10	28	31.4
Oil	294.0	19	40	265
	M_i	$M_i c_i$	$M_i h_i$	
Gas	1.329	2.793	8.244	
Oil	1.110	21.100	44.400	
		23.893	52.644	

Hence, according to the carbon atom-mol method:
$$\text{Gas cost} = \frac{2.793}{23.893} \times 100 = 11.7\%$$
and
$$\text{Crude cost} = 21.100/23.893 \times 100 = 88.3\%$$
according to the hydrogen atom-mol method:
$$\text{Gas cost} = \frac{8.244}{52.644} \times 100 = 15.7\%$$
and
$$\text{Crude cost} = \frac{44.40}{52.644} \times 100 = 84.3\%$$

10.8.C. Conclusion

The operationality of the atom-mol method is self-evident. We have delineated our choice alternatives to only two from among the several joint cost allocation methods presented hereinabove. A practical way of partially avoiding an arbitrary choice among these two methods is to take a simple average of the percentages arrived at by the two above-mentioned methods. This accommodates both of them for practical empirical application. Such average percentages will be used in the illustration presented in Chapter XIII.

CHAPTER XI

Royalties, Oil Inventories and the Cost of Goods Sold

THE DETERMINATION of an objective and equitable cost allocation method does not, by any means, dispel all the problems which face an international petroleum organization, nor does it ensure its survival. Of particular interest is the relationship of a foreign owned organization with exporting governments. The inherent problem of this relationship centers around the question of royalties. In our study we shall discuss the petroleum industry in the Middle East, where royalties are treated as payments on account of income tax due to an exporting government, or, in other words, as tax-credits. This procedure affects the total effective payments to the government by reducing the payments through an equivalent reduction in the tax paid. Although this practice is in accordance with present agreements, the Organization of Petroleum Exporting Countries has passed a resolution (IV. 33) which suggests that such royalties should be treated as expenses.

The fundamental difference in revenue returned to the exporting government may be illustrated by taking a simple royalty-tax calculation as an example. Suppose, then, the crude oil price is $1.80 a barrel, while the cost of production is $0.30 a barrel and the royalty is set at $0.30 a barrel. The net return to an exporting government would differ according to whether royalty is treated as an expense or as a tax-credit.

According to the present tax-credit basis, the government would receive $0.30 a barrel as that barrel is produced, but this return would not be treated as an expense. Thus,

Net income = $1.80 − $0.30 = $1.50;
Tax at 50% = $0.75; and
Tax payable = $0.75 − $0.30 = $0.45
Net effective receipts by government = ($0.45 + $0.30) or $0.75

In the OPEC proposed royalty-expensing basis, although the government still receive $0.30 per barrel as that barrel is produced, this amount is to be added to the cost of production. Thus,

Cost of production = $0.30 + $0.30 = $0.60;
Net income = $1.80 − $0.60 = $1.20; and
Tax at 50% = $0.60.

Then, the net effective receipts by the government are $0.30 royalty, and $0.60 tax. This is a total of $0.90, or $0.15 more for each barrel.

11.1. The Theory of Cost-Expense

Expenses are defined by the Committee on Concepts and Standards of the American Accounting Association as

> the expired costs directly or indirectly related to a given fiscal period, of the flow of goods or services into the market and of related operations.
> Expired costs are those having no discernible benefits to future operations.

The determination of the amount of royalty involved does not normally present a problem, since it is stated either in monetary units per ton or barrel (produced or sold) or as a percentage of the sales price. But the recognition of the time of expiration of costs is more complex, for it is not always certain whether it is a cost or not.

In certain cases royalties are paid to the owner of the land in kind, as a stated percentage of the oil produced. In effect, this means that they are an expense added to the cost of production, for they are incurred regardless of sale or profit. This is also true when royalties are paid in cash. In these cases, royalties are a pre-requisite expense, incurred before the sale, and, therefore, are part of the cost of production. In other cases, where the royalty is paid at the time of sale as a percentage of the sale price, it is a cost of goods sold. Yet, the cost incurred is fixed, and does not depend on whether the enterprise realized any profits.

In one case, the cost will not expire, and the expense is not incurred unless the goods are sold, while in the other, it is an expense all the time because it is paid before the goods are sold. In both cases it is not a profit item; it is either an unexpired cost or an expense. Therefore, net income, a difference between revenues and expenses of a given fiscal period, cannot be determined accurately unless all revenues and expenses, including royalties, are entered into the formula. If royalties are not calculated as an expense, costs are relatively understated and profits are overstated. Further, the use of the tax-credit method offsets the effect of the royalty payment to the producing government, because, through deduction from expenses, it reduces the income tax due. Whenever the income tax due is larger than the royalties paid we find that the government is, in effect, supplying the producing companies with oil free at the underground reservoir. In this case, oil is an inventory (an asset) rather than a cost of goods sold. Accordingly, we can look to the problem from two sides: We may say either that royalty is paid as a compensation to the owner for whatever was produced or sold, as if the company bought the oil from the owner (the government) at a stated price (royalty); or that the owner supplies that material at no charge (royalty), although it should be evaluated as an asset to present a more objective factual picture of the financial position of the enterprise. To refrain from doing so is to understate the assets, costs and expenses of the organization and correspondingly to overstate the profits.

11.2. Asset Value Measurement

The Committee on Concepts and Standards defines assets as economic resources devoted to business purposes within a specific accounting entity; they are aggregates of service potentials available for or beneficial to expected operations. Any increase or decrease in the aggregate amount of assets should be corroborated by a market transaction or its equivalent.[1]

This applies as far as the recognition of an asset is concerned with the

---

1. *Accounting and Reporting Standards ..., op. cit.*, pp. 13–4.

requirement of determining an objective measurement.[1] This measurement is a process of determining the money-equivalent of the asset's service potential, which is defined by the same group as

> the sum of the future market prices of all streams of service to be derived, discounted by probability and interest factors to their present worths.[2]

11.3. Assets of an International Petroleum Organization

We have discussed the current controversy connected with royalty expensing, and with this background in mind, we shall examine the assets of an international petroleum organization to see whether they are objectively identified and measured. We have been mainly occupied with the income statement, because of its prominence in the international oil controversies; yet, the balance sheet possesses equal importance, though not equal publicity. Quite often we read or hear the statement that oil producing companies (departments) obtain high rates of return on their investments in the producing countries. Indeed, it is estimated that

> As of the beginning of 1960, the total value of gross fixed assets in the petroleum industry of the world, excluding the Soviet bloc for which no data are available, was estimated at $97,250 million at historical costs, and the value of net fixed assets at $53,150 million.[3]

It is further estimated that 44.9% of the net fixed assets is tied to the production of crude oil.[4]

Because Venezuela and the Middle East are the two dominant exporters of oil for international trade, an evaluation of the enormous investments in these two areas seems to be in order. As of the beginning of 1960, the total value of gross fixed assets in these two areas was $10,250 million and the total value of net fixed assets was $5,825 million, while the net income was estimated to be $4,590 million for the year.[5]

---

1. *Ibid.*
2. *Ibid.*
3. Charles Issawi and Mohammed Yeganeh, *op. cit.*, p. 40.
4. *Ibid.*, p. 50.
5. *Ibid.*, pp. 41, 109.

Arthur D. Little, Inc., an American consulting firm, has made an attempt to demonstrate the distribution of profits between the various phases of the oil industry. The Shell paper has reported that, "according to press reports, this study claims that crude oil production in certain Middle East countries during the period of 1955–60 yielded 66% per annum on capital invested."[1] However, in the Shell opinion "66% is a high figure in anybody's language".[2]

We must decide whether the available figures of dollar values of assets, usually published balance sheet figures, actually reflect the values of all existing assets in the industry. It is a question of whether all existing assets have been recognized and measured properly; it has a bearing on periodic expense determination.

11.4. *Growth of an International Petroleum Organization*

A typical petroleum organization may begin one of its international production activities by acquiring a concession for exploration, development, production and exportation of crude oil and its derivatives somewhere in the Middle East, North Africa or Latin America. In the normal pattern, the organization starts with a certain amount of assets in the form of equipment and working capital, recorded on the balance sheet in the form of equity and loan capital. Table 11A portrays a simple balance sheet, which might be used by a new production department (subsidiary producing company) of an international petroleum organization at the inception of its operation in a producing country. It represents its financial position at that time, since it owns no petroleum reserves or oil inventories.

Table 11 A. 1.1 First Year

Assets		Liabilities	
Cash	XXX	Long-term loans	XXX
Materials	XXX	Equity-capital	XXX
Fixed Assets			
Exploration equipment	XXX		
Total assets	XXX	Total liabilities	XXX

---

1. *Petroleum Intelligence Weekly*, Special Supplement, Item 10, September 2, 1963, p. 12.
2. *Ibid.*

During the year activities take place in the form of geophysical surveys, either by the subsidiary itself, or by another specialized firm. Assuming that this subsidiary discovers oil, the company (producing department) defines the characteristics of the oil fields discovered and prepares for the start of production, since it now commands the oil reserves necessary to justify production.

After three years have elapsed, we find that little has changed other than the discovery and development of an oil field. It is, of course, an important occurrence in the history of the organization since it enables it to begin producing, selling and realizing profit. Nevertheless, such an important change in the financial position is not reflected in either the subsidiary or the organization on a balance-sheet at the end of year three. In fact, it is never reflected in the books of either entity. The balance-sheet of the subsidiary at that date may look like Table 11B,

Table 11B. 12.31 Of Year Three

Assets			Liabilities	
Cash		XXX	Current liabilities	XXX
Materials		XXX	Long-term loans	XXX
Fixed Assets			*Liabilities*	
Exploration equipment		XXX	Equity-capital	XXX
Production equipment and facilities	XXX			
Total assets		XXX	Total liabilities	XXX

We see that the balance sheet is designed to reflect the variation of one factor in the development of an oil producing company, assuming that all other things are equal. Balance-sheet terminology ignores the value of the discovered reserves. A more accurate representation of the situation at the end of year three is given by the balance-sheet in Table 11B₁.

Thus, the balance-sheet at the end of year three should reflect a value for the discovered hydrocarbon reserves as a part of the financial position of the enterprise, with a corresponding addition to the capital surplus. In essence, these new reserves are really new inventories; they are oil-in-place, for which a market price can be obtained. Table 11B, on the other hand, reflects the financial position of an oil company that has inventory to which no value has been assigned. Inventory is neither recognized nor measured, although the discovery of hydrocarbon reserves is clearly an addition to the "economic resources", assets devoted to "business purposes" within a part of the organization.[1] The hydrocarbon reserves (economic resources) command "aggregates of service potentials" and are, therefore, beneficial to expected operations.[2]

Subsequently, as the producing department of an international petroleum organization grows, the lack of recognition and measurement of reserves leads to greater understatement of assets (inventories), and of the cost of goods sold, and a resulting overstatement of periodic net income.

Table 11 B₁. 12.31 Of Year Three

Current Assets			Liabilities	
Cash	XXX		Current liabilities	XXX
Materials	XXX		Long-term loans	XXX
			Equity capital	XXX
Fixed Assets				
Exploration equipment	XXX			
Production equipment and facilities	XXX			
Subtotal	XXX		Subtotal	XXX
Plus			*Plus*	
Hydrocarbon reserves	XXX		Capital surplus	XXX
Total assets	XXX		Total liabilities	XXX

11.4. A. Value-measurement of Hydrocarbon Reserves

The discovery of new oil reserves is an addition to assets. In this, it resembles accretion, for it is not a direct function of exploration costs, but, rather of exploration risk. Exploration costs are incurred to find the oil, not to "manufacture" it. It is wealth uncovered. Professor Kuznets, in his *Economics of Change*, writes that the discovery of natural resources is a net addition to the national capital, in that it helps to increase the productivity of the economy. It does so in proportion to the assigned value of discovered resources. Accordingly, since no acquisition price exists for these oil

---

1. American Accounting Association, *op. cit.*,
2. *Ibid.*

reserves, the cost principle is not applicable. The only available method of measurement is the determination of the present worth of such reserves, which is derived from expected future prices and rates of interest. Although this makes the measured value rather uncertain, such reserves must be dealt with in this manner, for there seems to be no more satisfactory solution, for the measurement problem. Hence, the basis for valuation and measurement is taken to be the discounted present value of oil inventories.

11.4.B. Recognition and Measurement Limitations

The question of ownership of the oil is by no means clear, although generally it is a matter of special agreement between the producing government and the oil concessionaires. In Iran, for example, the government explicitly owns the underground oil reserves and "the consortium, the foreign element in Iranian oil operations, is not a concessionaire, but an operative agent on behalf of the Iranian State, the latter being the sole owner of its oil resources".[1] In this case the royalty paid is really a cost of goods sold or inventoried, and the treatment of royalties as credits to the income tax, rather than costs, would be an inaccurate accounting procedure. It is a stated payment to the owner of the oil extracted and, hence, a cost to the producing organization. To treat it otherwise would inflate net income and income tax due.

However, in the other agreements the provision for ownership of underground oil reserves by the state is not as clear. The standard provision in concession agreements includes "as a rule the exclusive right to explore, prospect, extract, refine and related matters (such as natural gas) within the area of the concession".[2] If these standard provisions are interpreted (legally) as rights to exploit resources for a limited period of time, while they continue to be owned by the state, the conclusion applying in the Iranian case is still valid. An owner receives a stated payment for every unit taken out of his vast reservoir, and this payment adds to the costs of goods sold or inventoried. Accordingly, net income is reduced. If this were practised, it would eliminate the necessity for evaluation of assets, and would mean that royalty payments could not be considered tax-credits. Applying the same rate of income tax will lead to more income to the government, through royalties, for it owns the resources; and through tax, for it is the sovereign tax collector. Necessarily,

---

1. George Lenczowski, *Oil and State in the Middle East* (Ithaca: Cornell University Press, 1960), p. 11.
2. *Ibid.*, p. 64

the treatment of royalty as cost would reduce taxable net income, but the net effect would be more money for government as a property owner and as a sovereign, and correspondingly less for the producing company. OPEC is asking to treat royalty as a price for the intrinsic value of oil, a cost of goods sold to the producer: an expense, not a tax credit.[1]

If the OPEC royalty resolution were adopted by governments and companies, the need for capitalizing oil reserves would be eliminated. The oil producing company would explore and discover oil on behalf of the producing government, and would purchase all or some of that oil when it needed it.

In theory, exporting governments and petroleum companies could agree to forego the royalty concept altogether. Then,

Table 11B_2. 12.31 of Year Three

Assets		Liabilities	
Cash	XXX	Current liabilities	XXX
Materials	XXX	Long-term loans	XXX
Fixed Assets		*Equity Capital*	
Exploration equipment	XXX	A shares	XXX
Production and equipment facilities	XXX	B shares	XXX
Subtotal	XXX		
Hydrocarbon reserves	XXX		
Total assets	XXX	Total liabilities	XXX

discovered oil reserves (belonging to the government) could be capitalized and recorded as capital subscription by the government in the producing company. Hence, Table 11B_1 would be transformed into Table 11B_2 as follows:

In this table the corresponding entry for the measured value of the hydrocarbon reserves discovered is the B shares while the original owners of the producing company are assigned the A shares which are equivalent

---

1. Shortly after this dissertation was submitted OPEC issued resolution VII.49 (7th Conference held in Djakar from 23rd to 28th November 1964) which resolved, among other things, the deletion of the royalty issue as was stated in resolution IU.33 (*op. cit.*, p. 69). The basic reason for this action was the acceptance by five OPEC members of royalty – expensing offers by some of the international oil companies.

to equity capital in Table 11B$_1$. Instead of assigning the corresponding entry to capital surplus, which belongs to the original owners of the producing company, this entry is made to equity capital (B shares). While foregoing royalties, the government would be a shareholder entitled to dividends on the B shares.

All discovered oil reserves, then, should be recognized and measured in order to portray more objectively the true value of the investment. If ownership is assigned legally to the oil producing company, the measured value of the oil reserve is then added to capital surplus. Otherwise, the government can consider this value as an addition to the national capital, or by agreement with the producing company, it can capitalize the value as a government share in the capital stock of the company, thereby eliminating royalty payments.

In the cases where reserves are capitalized within the producing company, regardless of the ownership of the reserves, the cost of production increases, due to the depletion of the reserves and the amortization of their capitalized value. This necessarily adds to the cost of production, and lowers net income and the rate of return on equity capital. Nevertheless, it is a necessary condition in order to determine an undistorted value for net income, since it more objectively portrays the financial position of the organization. The same condition applies, in a different manner, where no capitalization takes place and where royalties are not treated as an expense. In this case, royalties paid for oil and gas sold must be identified with the cost of goods sold. Those which are identified with inventories are product costs. Should the capitalized value of oil reserves be amortized at a per barrel rate equal to the present royalty payments, the net effect on costs and income would be the same, but not so on the distribution of profit, or on the payment for the capitalized reserves value, for if the ownership of reserves is assigned to the company, a stated cost for this ownership would probably be incurred. Otherwise, the government, as a major shareholder, is entitled to a substantial dividend, which would reduce profits available to original owners of the company.

Monetary recognition and measurement of oil reserves adds to cost of production, and, thereby reduces net income. It also adds to the equity capital, hence reducing the rate of return on that capital through a higher cost of production, higher capital investment and lower income.

Yet, through their presentation, we have seen that the available accounting decisions lead to the consistent answer once the per barrel amortization rate of the capitalized value of oil reserves is equal to the per barrel expensed royalty. Accordingly, since the available accounting decision alternatives are substantially equivalent in their contribution to a more objective expense and income calculation, both are equally satisfactory. Both would lead to identical outcomes at the present state of the royalty issue.

Accounting Theory of
the Neutral Value of Net Income

IN THE PREVIOUS part of this book we have been consistently referring to the accounting theory of the neutral value of net income. In particular, we postulated in Chapter IV that application of this theory would provide a survival value level for net income. Hence, it provides the value that a subset of the essential variables must take, in order that the survival equation can be solved to the satisfaction of the organization's goal.[1] This chapter covers the conceptual structure of the above-mentioned theory.

The application of this theory to a model of an international petroleum organization provides several more objective contributions to the recognition and measurement of revenues, expenses and assets. The theory in its abstract form is sufficiently flexible, however, to be applied to any other industry. Nevertheless, the new abstract premises are presented as logical constructs, while the problems and conditions prevailing in this industry provide some of the reasons underlying the form and substance of the theory. Hence, the theory in its abstract form is necessarily generalized, and, although it is capable of explaining and predicting accounting means and decisions in any industry, it still does not provide the practical technique of application. Thus, the particular empirical application derived from the abstract theory, introduced for the international petroleum industry, is similar to but not necessarily identical with particular empirical theories, which could be introduced for other industries. This lack of universality in the particular part of the theory is due to the structural differences encountered at times among the factors that dominantly affect the main variables in organizations

---

1. *Op. cit.*, Chapter 4.

belonging to different industries. As such, the peculiarities of each industry should be taken into consideration as far as their effect on accounting decisions is concerned.

In the international petroleum industry, as in many other industries, there are situations of conflict of interest. This is readily apparent in the question of the income of an oil producing company. Governments, owners, employees and others are continuously debating the profitability of this highly important industry. Whatever the specific context of the debate, it is linked to assets, revenues, or expenses; to the value of net income. This theory is the neutral judge, the impartial adjudicator. Its impartiality is derived from its objectivity and from its premises that are based on facts and on assumptions and techniques that are acceptable and applicable in mathematics and the natural sciences. It is a theory which is built on the logic of the sciences.

12.1. The Neutral Value of Net Income Underlying Abstract Premises

The theory of neutral value of income is built on two kinds of premises, abstract assumptions and empirical observations. Those explained in this section are abstract premises, without which the abstract basis of the theory could not have been developed. Premises of this kind do not change from one industry to another. They support the universal applicability of the theory. The empirical premises, those which are necessary for adaptation of the abstract part of the theory to the international petroleum industry, are discussed later. This is another area of differentiation between the neutral accounting theory and the conventional one. Accounting premises, called underlying concepts, have been elaborated by several authorities. They are mostly abstract premises related to the business entity, enterprise continuity, money measurement and realization. The neutral theory starts from these premises, taking the concepts of money measurement and realization as they have been defined by the Committee on Accounting Concepts and Standards of the AAA in 1957. However, it substitutes a wholly new and elaborate model for the business entity, of which continuity, through security and survival, is an integral portion. This is where the neutral accounting theory links with general organization theory. The conventional accounting theory does not have room for any particular industry as such; it is supposed to serve all industries. The neutral theory allows for the peculiarities of each industry to be considered through the availability of alternative accounting decisions. A rational choice is made among them, so that one which is characterized by the highest degree of objectivity will be chosen.

Furthermore, the neutral theory borrows two more abstract premises from other fields of knowledge and adapts them to accounting theory. The "limit" value of variables is taken from the field of mathematics, while the deductive logic is taken from the field of science and is incorporated into the philosophy of accounting methodology.

12.1. A. Rational Choice

The philosophy underlying the accounting neutral net income value theory is derived from the logic of the sciences. Accounting with its techniques, concepts and practices encounters problems which can be solved by none other than objective techniques. That is to say, a body of rationally delineated accounting concepts could provide the businessman with alternative accounting methods to choose from. To delineate such accounting decision alternatives, facts about the business entity must be known. The bookkeeping side of accounting provides a portion of these required facts as an integral part of the information-communication system of the business entity. Obviously, alternative accounting decisions lead to different outcomes, each affecting the objectives of the entity in a different manner.

In other words, the entity should know its internal and external environment and its position in such an environment as a necessary pre-requisite to delineating specific accounting methods and to making a choice among them. To do so, a criterion for choice must be established. Survival and security of the entity are taken to be its prime goal. To achieve this, business decisions most compatible with security and survival must be made continuously. Accounting decisions are only a portion of such business decisions, but they also must continuously be most compatible with its objective. It is a rational choice.

12.1. B. The Organization Model

An organization is a system of combined human and material objects interacting through an information decision-making mechanism, striving to survive within an environment constituted of factors directly and indirectly affecting what the organization is striving for. Its communication network receives, records and relays environmental information to the decision-making unit for action and counteraction to correct the values of its essential variables in a manner compatible with the organization's survival. The organization is equipped with governing mechanisms whose function is to achieve such correction. It is also equipped with a regulator, whose major work is to block the transmission of disturbances to the essential variables. Regulation may be imperfect, thus allowing, at times, complete or partial transmission of disturbances to the variables.

12.1.C. Value Measurement as a "limit"

Measured value, for our purposes, means a number that represents the quantification of an accounting datum. In many situations an exact measurement of values is possible, and whenever an exact measurement is impossible or unattainable, because of environmental disturbance, a value that approaches the exact value of accounting datum as a "limit" is chosen to be a satisfactory substitute. The word limit is taken in its general mathematical sense. In so far as the measured value of an accounting datum C approaches the exact value of datum C_i it is taken to be as exact value as possible under given circumstances.

12.1.D. Value Measurement in Terms of Money

The essential variables in the organization have numerical upper and lower limits against which the degree of success in maintaining the security of the organization is measured. The most common denominator for expressing accounting data used in such measurements within the environment of the organization is the monetary unit. Hence, money is the unit of measurement used in receiving, recording and relaying accounting information throughout the organization and its environment.

However, since the real value of money is a reflection of the price level, its expression varies according to changes in the level of prices. Hence, it is an imperfect measurement, as is clearly demonstrated when there are drastic fluctuations in the level of prices. Nevertheless, so long as the price level does not change drastically, the imperfect measurement is covered as a limit.

12.1.E. Value Recognition

Circumstantial, physical or conceptual evidence is a sufficient condition to substantiate the existence of accounting magnitudes, and, therefore, their recognition and communication to the governing mechanisms of the organization. It is left to the organization's decision-making unit to decide whether recognized magnitudes should be measured and made available to serve the organization's cause for legal or other reasons.

12.1.F. Definition of Accounting

Accounting is the discipline of receiving, recording in terms of money and communicating to the organization decision-making unit or units information about environmental occurrences affecting its essential variables; and of delineating alternative means of treating information as a basis for either choosing a fundamental method of action, or using such information for other managerial purposes related to its functioning. Thus, the science of accounting is divided into two basic divisions. On the one hand it states, tabulates and reports merely descriptive financial and cost information, constituted only of what are supposed to be bare facts about the environment of the organization. That it to say, it supplies undistorted information about the internal and external state with no analysis or delineation of alternative accounting treatment means. On the other hand, it enumerates and evaluates available means of treatment with a view to their contribution to the survival of the organization, or to any other subgoal for the organization.

Accounting offers a multitude of available methods, techniques, practices, and it makes available means of handling accounting data for whatever purposes such data are intended to be used. Some of these means may be appropriate at one time and compatible with choice criteria. The same means may not be so at another time, due to changes in the environment of the organization. Two means may be contradictory, if used simultaneously, although one could be appropriately chosen at one time, while the other could be chosen at another time. The only condition in choosing a set of means is consistency among them in the treatment of any one single accounting magnitude, as long as the set itself is consistent with the goal or subgoal strived for and contributes most favorably to it.

12.1.G. Net Income Formula

Accounting periodic net income is the numerical monetary difference between periodic revenues and expenses. It is a residuum formula. It is admitted that there are other net income formulae. However, this formula is chosen, by definition, as an integral part of premises constituting the abstract portion of the accounting theory of net income value neutrality.

12.1.H. The Neutral Value of Net Income: An Abstract Definition

The neutral value of net income for an organization in any one period is the constant monetary numerical difference between revenues and expenses identified with the period where

1. The organization's basic goal is survival.

2. Rational compatibility with this goal is the criterion for the choice among available revenue and expense measurement means.

3. Circumstantial physical or conceptual evidence is sufficient for substantiating recognition of the existence of revenues and expenses.

4. Limit value measurement of revenues and expenses is used only where exact measurement is impossible or unattainable because of environmental disturbances.

5. The measurement and entry of recognized revenues and expenses is a decision for the organization to make.

12.2. Theory of the Neutral Value of Net Income: The Empirical Particular Adaptation

We stated that the abstract and empirical portions of the theory are integral in any one single industry, and that the empirical particular portion could vary from one industry to another, depending on environmental variations among different industries, while the abstract portion is applicable totally or partially to all business organizations as long as there exists an adapted portion for the industry to which such an organization belongs.

In its adapted form, the theory accepts all the premises and definitions of the abstract theory, and deals with those aspects which are most relevant to the particular empirical case. In our study, these aspects represent the practical recognition and measurement of accounting data in the international petroleum industry. They deal with revenues, expenses and assets of an international petroleum organization. They are referred to hereafter as underlying particular premises.

12.2. A. Underlying Particular Premises

The adapted form of the theory is based on the following premises together with the basic abstract premises we have introduced.

1. Means of value measurement. The discipline of accounting is in possession of a wealth of measurement techniques, formulae, and more generally, measurement practices, which have been developed through the years to cope with the ever-increasing needs for measurement to solve problems of changing patterns. These means of measurement are based, in general, on cost or acquired values wherever expenses or assets are met. Occasionally, market considerations are introduced into a measurement technique. In the case of revenues, a realization test is used. At times, contradictory practices are available either to serve entirely different situations or to represent different judgments about measurement of accounting data. Yet, the adapted neutral net income value theory looks to available accounting techniques (means) to derive from them those techniques most compatible with the achievement of the organization's survival. In any one measurement problem, the theory postulates that there exists only one measurement technique (means) that satisfies the choice criterion.

In case none of the available accounting measurement means satisfies such a criterion, the theory permits the utilization of measurement means available in other sciences, particularly in economics.

2. Measurement of revenues. The problem of revenue measurement in the international oil industry is examined in detail in Chapter VII. There it is established that neither accounting nor market economics provides an exact revenue measurement due to the lack of arm's-length or freely competitive prices. Hence a limit value measurement means of revenues is borrowed from economic analysis to reflect a more objective description of sales transactions. Consequently, revenues of an international petroleum organization are measured through adjusted prices at any one export center for crude oil sold to customers in different market centers so that crude from any export area could be delivered in that market at an equal price. The difference in transportation costs is taken as an adjustment in the F.O.B. price. This makes sales prices in any one market center equal to the highest price in the said market center.

(a) *Definition of a market center.* A market center is defined for revenue measurement purposes as one in which none of the existing petroleum suppliers can be spared out of that market at the period under examination, for economic or other reasons. Further, petroleum provided by the highest price supplier must be in quantities "material" enough in comparison with the quantity of petroleum provided to the same market by other suppliers. Materiality here is interpreted in its general conventional accounting sense.

3. Averaging of joint production and pre-production costs. Joint costs are defined as those costs incurred for the finding and production of several hydrocarbon elements in uncontrollable proportions. These elements are grouped for practical purposes into two basic categories, liquid and gaseous hydrocarbon elements, crude oil and natural gas. In Chapters VIII and IX we analyzed several joint cost averaging methods, and established that the mixed hydrocarbon method produces a satisfactory approximation of average pre-production and production costs for oil and gas, on a limit value basis. The method developed in this study is a weighted average of the pure carbon atom and the pure hydrogen atom methods, which are defined as being more exact and reflective of actual situations than any other method.

4. Identifiable costs. The premise of identifiable costs is substantially the same as the conventional accounting concept of not expensing in any one accounting period, but the expiring costs of that period. In other words, it calls for the capitalization of the costs which are related to future periods. More specifically, in an international petroleum organization, a categorization of these costs is necessary.

(a) *Exploration casts.* Productive exploration costs are to be capitalized and depleted on a unit of production basis, which is the most approximate representation of existing situations. Thus, incurred expenditures are divided in a capitalized form between underground reserves of hydrocarbon liquids and gases according to the atom-mol method.

(b) *Drilling and development costs.* The costs of drilling and development are incurred after oil and gas have been discovered, and prepare the field for actual production. Any tangible production facility existing as a result of these tangible and intangible costs has a productive life. Hence, capitalization is called for, together with a unit of production depreciation. If oil and gas are produced together, as occurs in most cases, unit costs are to be divided between them according to the atom-mol method.

(c) *Operating and general costs of hydrocarbon production.* After the two stages of exploration and development are over, other direct and indirect operating costs are incurred. These costs are identified with the hydrocarbons produced in any one accounting period. They are product costs to be inventoried whenever the hydrocarbons are not sold in that period. Again, if oil and gas are produced jointly, the costs are divided between them according to the averaging method we have advocated.

(d) *Periodic expense measurement.* The outcome of the joint costs averaging and the identifiable costs determination is periodic expense limit measurement. The capitalization and unit of production depletion-amortization-depreciation are well known accounting techniques, but they are not applied in most international petroleum organizations. The method of hydrocarbon atom-mol averaging of costs, proper capitalization and a unit of production depletion-amortization-depreciation procedure, which we have found to be more objective than other available accounting means, are chosen as a prime condition in the determination of a neutral value of net income. Periodic or product non-joint expenses that lend themselves to exact measurement are charged accordingly.

5. *Measurement of assets and inventories.* The discovery of new oil reserves within a country is an addition to its national wealth, through its contribution to the increase in the economic resources available to the organization that made the discovery. For the discovered resources no acquisition price exists to provide an exact basis for measurement. Furthermore, because no market place for the whole reserves exists to provide another measurement yardstick, the discounted present value of the reserves is a limit substitute measurement basis. Should an organizational decision be made to measure the reserves and to record them as inventories, the present value is the limit measured value to be used. But, if this is not done, the royalties paid should

be dealt with as product costs, in order to arrive at an undistorted value for net income.

12.2.B The Neutral Value of Net Income. An Empirical Particular Definition

The neutral value of net income for an international petroleum organization in any one period is the constant monetary numerical difference between revenues and expenses identified with said period where

1. The abstract definition of the neutral value of net income is considered as given.

2. The value measurement means available in accounting, as well as in other fields of knowledge, constitutes a pool of alternatives for choosing those which satisfy a choice criterion.

3. F.O.B. prices are adjusted in a way that the delivered (C.I.F.) price in any market center is equal to the highest prevailing delivered price in that market.

3a. A market center is one in which none of the existing relatively important suppliers can be spared because of economic or other reasons.

4. The averaging of production and pre-production costs is made in accordance with the atom-mol method.

5. Exploration costs are capitalized and divided among quantities of underground hydrocarbon reserves according to the hydrocarbon atom-mol method and depleted according to a unit of production basis.

6. Drilling and development costs are capitalized and depreciated or amortized according to a unit of production basis.

7. Operating and general costs of hydrocarbon production are treated as product costs, while the division of these costs, in case of joint production of oil and gas, are made according to the averaging method we have defined.

8. Other non-joint periodic expenses or product costs that lend themselves to exact measurement are charged accordingly.

9. Underground hydrocarbon reserves are recognized and measured according to their discounted present value and amortized periodically as product costs, or if not so recognized, then the royalties paid are treated as product costs.

CHAPTER XIII

The Neutral Value of Net Income: A Partially Empirical Illustration

13.1. Introduction

THE CHASE MANHATTAN BANK of New York issues an annual financial economic study called *Petroleum Industry 19–*. This study for 1961 covers the operations of 33 oil companies which, in the Bank's judgment, are representatives of the whole oil industry. Table 13A illustrates the combined statement of financial position and Table 13B shows the combined state of income as reported in the study. The measurement of the data presented in tables 13A and 13B was made according to the conventional measurement techniques. The theory of the neutral value of net income calls for measurement techniques different from those used in the construction of Tables 13A and 13B. To compare the outcome of these different measurement techniques more properly requires much more original data than those available to us.

Table 13A
Combined Statement of Financial Position
December 31, 1961

Millions of US dollars

Current assets	13,744	13,744
Less current liabilities	5,836	5,836
Net working capital	7,908	
Property plant and equipment	53,163	
Less accumulated depreciation	25,924	

Net plant and equipment	27,339	27,339
Other assets and deferred charges		
Investments and advances	2,137	
Long-term receivables	596	
Special funds and deposits	70	
Pre-paid charges and other assets	440	
Total other assets and deferred charges	3,247	3,247
Net assets		44,330
Other liabilities		
Long-term debt	4,936	
Deferred credits	580	
Other reserves	736	
Minority interests	625	
Total other liabilities	6,877	6,877
Total current and other liabilities	12,713	
Net worth		
Preferred stock	241	
Common stock capital surplus	12,968	
Earnings re-invested in business	18,408	
Shareholders' equity	31,617	31,617
Total liabilities and net worth		44,330

Table 13 B
Combined Statement of Income for the Year Ended
December 31, 1961

	Millions of U.S. dollars	
Gross operating income	33,784	
Non-operating income	792	
Total income	34,576	34,576
Operating costs and expenses	25,804	
Taxes – other than income taxes	1,175	
Depreciation, depletion, amortization and retirements	3,237	
Interest expense	227	
Other charges	7	

Total deductions	30,451	30,451
Net income before income taxes		4,125
Estimated income taxes	980	
Income applicable to minority interest	<u>64</u>	
	<u>1,044</u>	<u>1,044</u>
Net income		<u>3,081</u>

A comparison is made through adjusting the data of Tables 13A and 13B to conform as much as possible to the requirements of the theory of the neutral value of net income. In this adjustment process some approximations and hypothetical assumptions are necessary because of the lack of an original and complete set of data. In any practical case, such approximations and assumptions would be completely unnecessary. Moreover, although the data is not for one company, we shall deal with it as if it were. For these reasons, the illustration is only partially empirical. Consequently, the numerical illustration requires the introduction of a measurement correction factor to adjust the data in Tables 13A and 13B whose measurement does not wholly conform to the requirements of our theory. New adjusted statements are drawn to provide for measurement corrections.

In this illustration, only the production stage is considered, since it provides an area where the application and contribution of the income neutrality theory is most apparent. We must, then, restate Tables 13A and 13B so that they contain data on the production stage only. Tables 13C and 13D reflect this restatement of revenues and expenses of the combined operations of the 33 oil companies as they are allocated to the production stage. This proration starts from factual statements, but uses certain underlying assumptions (which are given as footnotes to Table 13D). These assumptions, though basically illustrative, lead, in an explanatory manner, to revenues, assets, and expenses that are reasonably close to the actual figures. Without access to original detailed data, it is impossible to determine how close these figures are to the actual figures. The only proof available is the degree of objectivity inherent in the underlying proration assumptions. We can be sure, however, that production revenue figures are as accurate as they can be without access to original data since prices and transportation expenses are published and available. Production costs are also typical of known and published figures, both in the Middle East and Venezuela. In the tables and footnotes supplied throughout this illustration, enough published data is provided to substantiate these assertions.

The proration of assets, equity capital, liabilities, and other data, exclusive of proven hydrocarbon reserves, cannot be represented as accurately, but the values of proven hydrocarbon reserves are available and published in so many sources that substantiation is not needed.

Of course, under practical conditions production subsidiaries have their own records as a source of data and no need for assumptions arises.

13.2. Production Revenues

To arrive at production revenues, we must obtain information regarding the quantity of hydrocarbons produced. Furthermore, information about prices and other basic assumptions is also required. Production and price data, together with the basic assumptions, are dealt with in the sections which follow.

13.2. A. Hydrocarbon Production

According to the Chase study for 1961, total crude oil production for the 33 companies was 10,819 thousand barrels per day (T.B.D.) or 3,948,945 thousand barrels per year. From this amount 6,309 T.B.D. or 2,302,795 thousand barrels per year were produced outside the United States.

13.2. B. Export Prices

Export prices through the main crude oil export centers in the period from 1959 to 1961 were as follows:

Neutral Value of Net Income
Middle Eastern, United States and Venezuelan Ports
Years 1959–1961

Country	Outlet	Ports	API gravity of crude petroleum in degrees	1959 U.S. $	1960 U.S. $	1961 U.S. $
Iran	Persian Gulf	Bunder Meshhur	34	1.88	1.84	1.78
Iraq	Persian Gulf	Fao	36	1.82	1.78	1.72

Country	Outlet	Ports	API gravity of crude petroleum in degrees	1959 U.S. $	1960 U.S. $	1961 U.S. $
Iraq	Mediterranean	Tripoli	36	2.33	2.28	2.21
Kuwait	Persian Gulf	Ahmadi	32	1.69	1.65	1.59
Neutral Zone	Persian Gulf	Mina Saud	24	1.51	1.49	1.48
Qatar	Persian Gulf	Umm Said	39	2.05	1.98	1.91
Saudi Arabia	Persian Gulf	Ras Tannura	34	1.90	1.87	1.80
Saudi Arabia	Mediterranean	Sidon	34	2.29	2.24	2.17
U.S.	Gulf Coast		34	3.28	3.28	3.28
Venezuela	Carribbean Sea	Puerto la Cruz	36	2.84	2.80	2.80

Source: Charles Issawi and Mohammed Yeganeh, *Economics of Middle Eastern Oil*, Faber and Faber, London 1962, p. 681 (Table 21).

13.2.C. Basic Assumptions

The basic assumptions regarding revenue are as follows:

1. Crude oil produced from the U.S. is priced at the average Gulf Coast posted price of 1961, namely $3.28 per barrel, for a production of 1,646,150 thousand barrels per year (T.B.Y.) in the same year.

2. Crude oil produced in the rest of the Western Hemisphere is priced at the average Caribbean Sea posted price for 1961, $2,80 per barrel, for a production of 976,740 T.B.Y. in the same year.

3. Crude oil produced in the Eastern Hemisphere is priced at the average of Persian Gulf posted prices for 1961, that is $1.71 per barrel for a production of 1,326,045 T.B.Y. for the same year.

13.2 D. Production Costs and Other Expenses

To arrive at production cost and to determine other expenses, information regarding investment in production operations and cost of petroleum operations is required; thus, we must determine depreciation and operating costs. This information is dealt with as follows.

(a)   Depreciation, depletion, amortization, and retirements are prorated to production according to the percentage of investment in fixed assets in production to total gross investment in fixed assets in all phases in 1961. This percentage is 54.1% of $3,237 million, or $1, 51 million.

(b)   Cost of petroleum operations in the period 1958–1960 is estimated by Issawi and Yeganeh to be:

	Middle East			Venezuela		
	1958	1959	1960	1958	1959	1960
Cost of petroleum operation in $M	491	552	575	992	1014	1000

(c)   Depreciation figures are available up to 1958 for the Middle East. They average about 27% of cost of petroleum operations in the period 1948–1958, being somewhat higher towards the end of the period. If we take the years 1956–8 as a representative period, we find that the average is 28%. Accordingly, depreciation charges are assumed to be 28% of the costs of petroleum operation in the Middle East.

(d)   For Venezuela, comparable percentages are not available. In order to derive operating costs and expenses for all production of oil outside the United States, a per-unit cost, excluding depreciation (calculated according to the Middle East ratios explained previously), will be calculated and applied. We assume that Venezuelan per-unit operating costs and expenses apply to Western Hemisphere production outside the U. S., and that Middle East operating costs apply to Eastern Hemisphere production.

(e)   Gross crude oil production of the 33 oil companies, included in our study came from the following geographical areas:

Area	1961 (T.B.D.)	Total 1961 per area (T.B.Y.)
United States	4,510	1,646,150
Other Western Hemisphere	2,676	976,740
Eastern Hemisphere	3,633	1,326,045
Total worldwide	10,819	3,948,935

(f)   Unit operating costs are calculated as follows:

	Middle East	Venezuela
	(in millions)	
Cost of petroleum operations, 1958–60	$1,618	$2,006
Less average depreciation (28% of total operating expenses)	453	562
Cost of petroleum operations	$1,165	$1,444
Total production, 1958–60 (TB)	5,157,810	3,001,030
Unit operating cost (per barrel)	$0.21	$0.48
Unit depreciation (per barrel)	$0.09	$0.15

(g)   Issawi and Yeganeh report that the average cost of crude oil production in recent years has been about $1.75 in the United States.

(h)   The $1.75 production cost per barrel for the U.S. appears to include depreciation, and it is used as such for the purposes of this illustration.

13.2.ℰ. *Production Assets and Liabilities*

The Chase study calculates the net assets devoted to hydrocarbon production to be $44,180 million. This figure is used to represent net plant and equipment in Table 13C. Assuming that the percentage of net plant and equipment to total net assets in all phases to be the same as the one in production, we find that the $14,180 million represents 61.7% of total net assets in production. If these assets are prorated accordingly, we find that $22,982 million is devoted to production. Other assets are calculated in the same manner.

Total liabilities and net worth are derived from total assets. The percentages are maintained at the same level as those in integrated operation.

Table 13C
Combined Statement of Financial Position
(Crude-Oil Production Phase Only)
December 31, 1961

	(Millions of U.S. $)		
	X Percentage of all assets	Y All phases	Z Production
Current assets	31.0	13,744	7,124 ([a])
Net plant and equipment	61.7	27,339	14,180 ([c])
Deferred charges and other assets	7.3	3,247	1,678 ([b])
Total	*100*	*44,330*	*22,982*
Current liabilities	13	5,836	2,988 ([d])
Other liabilities	16	6,877	3,677 ([e])
Shareholders' equity	71	31,617	16,317 ([f])
Total	*100*	*44,330*	*22,982*

([a, b]) Estimated according to the percentages in column X to the total net assets in the production phase, since reliable data is not available.

([c]) This figure is given by the Chase Manhattan Bank and is taken from the same source referred to previously (p. 41).

([d, e, f]) These figures are a reflection of the assumption that production operations have the same relationship of equity capital to total assets as prevailing in integrated operation.

Table 13 D
Combined Statement of Income (Crude-Oil Production Phase Only) (ᵃ)
(For The Year Ended December 31, 1961)

	Millions of U.S. $	
Gross operating income		
U.S. production: 1,646,150 TB/year @ $3.28 per barrel	5399	
Remaining Western Hemisphere: 976,740 TB/year @ $2.80 per barrel	2730	
Eastern Hemisphere: 1,326,045 TB/year @ $1.71 per barrel	2268	10,297
Natural gas sales		1,156
Total gross operating income		11,553
Operating cost and expenses		
U.S. production cost, inclusive of depreciation ($1.75 per barrel)	2,881	
Other Western Hemisphere: production cost, exclusive of depreciation ($0.48 per barrel)	469	
Eastern Hemisphere: production cost, exclusive of depreciation ($0.21 per barrel)	278	
Total operating costs and expenses		3,628
Depreciation, depletion, amortization and retirements		
U.S. production	–	
Other Western Hemisphere ($0.15 per barrel)	147	
Eastern Hemisphere, ($0.09 per barrel)	119	
Total production cost	3,894	
Total depreciation etc.	266	
Other charges and deductions (prorated 52.48% in favor of production)(ᵇ)	733	
Total all deductions	4,627	
Net income before income taxes and royalties	6,926	

(ᵃ) All these figures are derived on the assumption that all crude-oil refined is transferred from production, the rest being sold as crude. The crude oil revenue is supposed to reflect this assumption, which cannot be substantiated, but which seems reasonable in the light of the nature of the operations conducted.

(ᵇ) This is the ratio of (i) investment in fixed assets related to production to (ii) total investment, both as of December 31, 1961.

13.3. The *Measurement* *Adjustment* Process

In this illustration the only adjustment that has been necessary has been for arriving at data related to the production phase only. This phase was chosen because it reflected the distorting factors, which we have discussed, directly and clearly. Furthermore, almost all the significant controversies which affect the survival of the organization occur in this stage. In this section of the illustration application of the theory of the neutral value of net income shall take place through adjustment in the measured data derived from the premises of the theory and from its empirical particular conditions. The measurement adjustment process shall be applied to some of the items constituting Tables 13C and 13D. The outcome will be tabulated in Tables 13E and 13F.

13.3. *A. Revenue Measurement*

The world-wide combined operations of 33 oil companies, including five out of the seven international majors, sell more oil in the form of crude and refined products than their crude production, a fact, at least, for the year 1961 as reported in the Chase study. This means that they are net buyers of crude oil, despite their own vast sources of supply, which constituted more than 52% of 1961 crude oil production in the free world. The percentage of crude sales outside any one affiliated group, although never clearly indicated, is known to be a rather small percentage. These third party sales, as they are called, are usually minimal. Of course, it is only logical that they must first satisfy their own needs in refining and marketing, before they sell to others. Furthermore, the producing subsidiaries do not really have the option of selling in the general market or to non-affiliates, but, instead, must transfer their production to the parent companies, or their marketing and refining affiliates. Consequently, their production is transferred rather than sold to them by their producing subsidiaries. This is a further evidence of the lack of significant independent sales to establish a yardstick of an arm's-length price.

However, a price is definitely necessary in practice, since there are groups interested in production profits who are not interested in other stages of operations. The only available means of investigation is an examination of market prices or a near approximation thereof. In the example under consideration, there are three sources of production: the United States, the rest of the Western Hemisphere, and the Eastern Hemisphere. There are different published and prevailing prices in each of the three areas. Under competitive conditions, and with sufficient production capacity in the low cost areas, the marginal high cost producers would be driven out of the market. However, since the conditions of competition do not really prevail, low and high cost producers can exist in line with high and low prices. In fact, some of the major oil companies produce simultaneously from both high and low cost areas and transfer their production at different prices. Assuming that the main market of Western Hemisphere crude of this group is the United States, and assuming that freight charges equal the difference between U.S. delivered price and the Venezuelan F.O.B. price, then we may conclude that all Western Hemisphere production is essentially priced at the U.S. price of $3.28 per barrel. Accordingly, if freight charges average $0.48 a barrel in the Western Hemisphere for all oil produced excluding the U.S., this $0.48 must be added as a cost and a revenue at the same time. This factor, then, has no effect on net profit, but it illustrates the point. If the group is operating exclusively in the Western Hemisphere, the $3.28 per barrel might have been considered a good indication of the size of an arm's-length price. If the Eastern Hemisphere were treated in the same manner, and if the freight charges to the U.S. Gulf Coast were $1.57 per barrel, which would make the delivered price in the U.S. equal to $3.28 per barrel, then both the $1.71 and the $2.80 of Eastern and Western Hemisphere might be indicative of an arm's-length price.

None of this is realistic, however, since the U.S. does not constitute the whole market of the group. Furthermore, freight charges are quite different from what we have assumed above. At scale-10%[1] the transportation cost from Venezuela to New York is $0.31 per barrel and $1.11 from the Persian Gulf to the same destination.

The theory of the neutral value of net income requires an adjustment of F.O.B. prices in a way that delivered (C.I.F.) prices in any one market are equal to the delivered prices of the most inefficient producer. To apply this condition of the theory, we shall assume that there are only two distinct markets for the combined operations of these 33 oil companies, the U.S. and Europe. Furthermore, we shall assume that the U.S. crude production will be consumed first, before any foreign crude is imported. Thus, if their domestic market is commensurate with their refining throughput in the U.S., we find

---

1. The tanker rate structure is explained in J. Bes, *Tanker Shipping*, Drukkerij V./H. C. de Boer Jr. (Hilversum, Netherlands, 1963).

that 7,168 T.B.D. is used, the rest, 3651 T.B.D., is marketed in Europe. The figure of 7,168 T.B.D. is derived as follows: 4,510 T.B.D., their total U. S. production; 408 T.B.D., their Canadian production; 2,054 T.B.D., their Venezuelan production; 196 T.B.D., their Western Hemisphere production; thus, 7168 T.B.D. is the total market. We assume that their European market is supplied from their Eastern Hemisphere production.

13.3. B. Price Adjustment for the Two Markets

If we treat Canadian production as a part of U.S. production, we find that the total quantities domestically produced and transferred for processing in 1961 were 1,795,070,000 barrels priced at the U.S. Gulf Coast published price of $3.28 per barrel, and produced $5,887,829,600 in revenues. If we deduct from the U.S. Gulf Coast price of $3.28 the transportation charge (at scale 3–10%) of $0.31 to New York, we find an adjusted F.O.B. price in Venezuela of $2.97 per barrel. This produces $2,226,638,700 in revenues for a production of 749,710,000 barrels in 1961. And, if we deduct from the U.S. Gulf Coast price of $3.28 the transportation charge (at scale 3–10%) of $1.11 to New York, we derive an adjusted F.O.B. Persian Gulf price of $2.17 per barrel. This produces $155,241, 800 of revenues from crude imported to the U.S. from the Eastern Hemisphere in 1961, for a production of 71,540,000 barrels. The total adjusted production revenues for 1961, then, are $ 8,269,710,100 from selling in the U.S. market.

The most inefficient producer selling in the European market is Venezuela, whose oil is delivered in London at a price of $3.32 (F.O.B., price $2.80 + $0.52 and transportation to London at scale 3–10%). The application of the revenue measurement adjusts the F.O.B. price, so that the delivered price in London will be the same. Hence, deducting (at scale 3–10%) a transportation charge of $0.92 a barrel from the Persian Gulf to London produces an adjusted F.O.B. Persian Gulf price of $2.40 a barrel. Assuming, for purposes of the illustration, that the entire European market is served from London, the production revenues would then be $3,198,276,000 for 1961 for a production of 1,332,615,000 barrels. Thus, the total adjusted production revenues for 1961 are $11,467,985,500 as compared with $10,397,000,000 exclusive of sales of natural gas, a difference of well over a billion dollars. Adding $1,156,000,000 reported revenues (without any adjustment) from natural gas, we arrive at a total adjusted production revenue of $12,623,985,500.

13.3.C. Expense Measurement

The theory of the neutral value of net income applies different means of measurement of periodic expenses to those applied generally by the international petroleum industry. The two prime considerations have been the allocation of joint costs and the adjustment for the capitalization effect.

13.3.D. Exploration and Development Expenses

Exploration and development expenditures incurred by the group are available in the study since 1957 as follows:

Year	million dollars
1957	3877
1958	3141
1959	3309
1960	3192
1961	3295
Total	16,814

It is also reported that the following expenditures from this category have been charged to income in 1961:

	million dollars
Intangible development costs (not capitalized)	38
Dry hole cost (not capitalized)	349
Exploration expenditures charged to income	619
Total	1,006

This represents about 32% of the total spending on exploration and development in 1961. The assumption that identical percentages of these expenditures have been charged to income in the previous years, leads to the following tabulation. (See following page).

The total of $5,332 million is to be capitalized and amortized on a unit of production basis. That is a requirement of the theory on the assumption that the group started operation in 1957. To calculate a unit of production amortization of such expenditures, we must have information with regard to the oil and gas reserves discovered and production since 1957. Because

Year	Capitalized	Expensed	Total
1957	2636	1241	3877
1958	2136	1005	3141
1959	2250	1059	3309
1960	2171	1021	3192
1961	2289	1006	3295
Total (in millions of $)	11,482	5332	16,814

information about reserves is not available in the study, we must use approximate figures. Reserves and production figures are tabulated as follows:

Year	Additions to reserves (in billions of barrels)	Assumed production (in millions of barrels)
1957	10	3311
1958	10	3289
1959	10	3510
1960	10	3728
1961	10	3948
Total	*50*	*17,786*
1957 endowment	150	(accumulated production)
Total	*200* (accumulated reserves)	

Furthermore, we assumed that the group was endowed with another 150 billion barrels in 1957, roughly 58% of the free world reserves at that time.

To sum up our figures, we have recorded 200 billion barrels of accumulated reserves and about 18 billion barrels of accumulated production, with an accumulated exploration and development expenditure of $17 billion. Of this, about $11 billion was already capitalized. Our theory calls for the capitalization of the rest. Part of the capitalized portion has been amortized in previous years including 1961.

A unit of production amortization is required. In this illustration it is an average for the years 1947–61 as an expediency. The total of $17 billion of exploration expenditure is necessarily a joint cost, for oil and gas. A total of 50 billion barrels of oil was discovered. An assumed figure for gas is used on the basis of 500 standard cubic feet (S.C.F.) of gas associated with every barrel of oil. This means about 25 billion M.S.C.F. of gas.

According to the average of the atom-mol method of allocating joint cost 86.3% would be allocated to oil and 13.7% to gas. Hence $2,304 million is allocated to gas and $14,510 million to oil. Averaged over all the oil and gas discovered, a unit of cost of $0.2775 per barrel of oil and $0.0441 per M.S.C.F. of gas, is obtained. The exploration unit cost for oil is rather high because about 75% of the expenditures incurred were in the U.S. where oil is no longer found in abundant quantities. However, these figures are only illustrative and should not be interpreted otherwise.

13.3.E. Exploration and Development Expense, 1961

For a production of 3,948 million barrels of oil, a total amortized exploration expense would be $1,263 million, and for a production of 1,972 million M.S.C.F. of gas an amortized exploration expense of about $3 million is obtained. However, since $1,006 has already been charged in Table 13C, only the difference of $260 million will be charged in Table 13F. In order to calculate at the end of 1961 the un-amortized part of exploration expenditures, the previous year's production must be considered. From 1957 to the end of 1960 the group produced 13,739 million barrels of oil and 6,869 million M.S.C.F. of gas. Hence, it amortized $4,416 million for oil and $11 million for gas. The total accumulated amortization for exploration expenditures, then, is $5,666 million. Accordingly, the balance sheet of 1961 should record $11,148 million of un-amortized exploration expenditures.

13.3.F. Operating and General Costs of Production

In Table 13D operating and general expenses were assigned to crude oil. None were assigned to natural gas. When we allocate these costs according to the mixed hydrocarbon atom method, we find that out of a total production cost of $3,894 million, $3,803 is allocated to oil and $91 million to gas. This would not affect the ultimate calculation of the neutral value of net income, as was the case for exploration cost. Nonetheless, it provides a more objective measurement of product costs.

13.3.G. *Fixed Inventories or Royalty Expensing*

For illustrative purposes only, we shall assume that the group has only 20 billion barrels of reserves in the United States out of the 182 billion barrels available to it at the end of 1961. Furthermore, we shall assume that these 20 billion barrels are owned by the group, while the other 162 billion belong to foreign governments who collect an average $0.25 royalty per barrel of crude produced, and, finally, that the group does not have any beginning or closing inventories. When we apply the theory of the neutral value of net income, the discounted present value of the 20 billion barrels of oil and the 10 billion M.S.C.F of gas must be recognized and recorded.

The discounted present value of a barrel of oil is assumed to be $1 and of a thousand S.C.F. of gas $0.01. Hence, the added values to Table 13E for fixed inventories of oil and gas are $20 billion and $100 million.

Royalties on gas are assumed to be "nil", while royalties on the 2,303 million barrels produced outside the U.S. are calculated at $0.25 million for 1961. This is an added expense to the 1961 production, since adjusted Table 13D figures are exclusive of royalties. Furthermore, a depletion provision for oil produced in the U.S. on the basis of one U.S. dollar per barrel is required on the assumption that the 20 billion barrel oil reserves were 21,646,150 T.B. on January 1, 1961. No changes in the present value of oil or gas reserves are considered. Hence, the depletion expense would be $1,646 million for the oil produced. Treating gas in the same manner, the depletion expense would be $8 million. This completed the application of the theory of neutral value of net income to the combined income figures of a group of 33 oil companies in an illustrative manner. The outcome of the application is tabulated in Tables 13E and 13F in a comparative manner with re-classified data from Tables 13C and 13D.

Table 13E
Combined Statement of Financial Position, December 31, 1961
(Crude Oil and Natural Gas Production Phase)

	Millions of U.S. dollars		
	All phases unadjusted	Production unadjusted	Production adjusted
Current assets	13,744	7124	7124
Net plant and equipment	27,339	14,810	14,180
Deferred charges and other assets	3247	1678	1678
Investment in exploration	–	–	11,148
Fixed inventories	–	–	20,100
Total	44,300	22,982	54,230
Current liabilities	5836	2988	2988
Other liabilities	6877	3677	3677
Capital surplus	–	–	31,248
Shareholders equity	31,617	16,317	16,317
Total	44,330	29,982	54,230

Table 13F
Combined Statement of Income on December 31, 1961
(Crude Oil And Natural Gas Production Phase)

	Millions of U.S. dollars	
Gross Operating Income	Production unadjusted	Production adjusted
U.S. and Canadian production 1,795,070 T.B. at $3.28 per barrel		5888
Venezuelan production 749,710 T.B. exported to U.S. at $2.97 per barrel		2227
Eastern Hemisphere production 71,540 T.B. exported to U.S. at $2.17 per barrel		155
Total revenues from U.S. market		8270
Eastern Hemisphere Production 1,332,615 T.B. at $2.40 per barrel		3198

Gross Operating Income	Millions of U.S. dollars	
	Production unadjusted	Production adjusted
Total crude production revenue	10,397	11,468
Natural gas sales	1156	1156
TOTAL GROSS OPERATING INCOME	11,553	12,624
Operating Costs and Expenses		
U.S. production at $1.75 per barrel	2881	
Other Western Hemisphere production at $0.63 per barrel		
Eastern Hemisphere production at $0.30 per barrel	397	
Total crude oil general and operating production cost	3,894	3,803
Total natural gas general and operating production cost	–	91
Amortization of investment in exploration at $0.2775 per barrel and $0.0441 per M.S.C.F. of gas produced	–	260
Royalties on oil produced outside the U.S.	–	576
Depletion expense (oil)	–	1,646
Depletion expense (gas)	–	8
Total operating costs and expenses	3,894	6,384
Other charges and deductions	733	733
Grand total all deductions	4,627	7,117
Net income	6,926	
Neutral value of net income		5,507

Analogue of a Purposive System of Human Behavior (Concluding Summations and Extensions)

14.1 Systems

THE PRECEDING study of accounting and business organization can be described in terms of a purposive system of organizational behavior. A system in this sense reflects a "cohesive collection" of things in a "connective" form.[1] Systems of this kind "can be pointed out as aggregates of bits and pieces; but they begin to be understood only when the connections between the bits and the pieces, the dynamic interactions of the whole organism, are made the object of study".[2] This is the first lead to our approach in assessing accounting for income determination in the oil industry. An oil company can be looked at as a system consisting of a number of elements. Such elements must be investigated, wholly or partially, depending on the ultimate purpose of the study, before that purpose can be achieved in a rational and objective manner. Only in this manner can problems of survival-oriented regulation, and control be handled more effectively, including those that relate to the gathering, formulation, and communication of information regarding the behavior of the system and its elements.

A manager receiving the various sorts of information through the system's communication networks makes a decision even if "he has decided by default not to decide".[3] In other words, he exercises a choice within a

---

1. Stafford Beer, *Cybernetics and Management* (London: The English University Press, 1960), p. 39.
2. *Ibid.*, p. 9.
3. *Ibid.*, p. 11.

certain frame of reference based on the information conveyed to him. The accounting discipline is an integral part of the organization's information-communication network. Recognition and measurement of net income determinants were analyzed on the basis of the exercise of choice according to certain established criteria. This is only a statement of the problem from a different perspective.

14.2. Purposive Systems

A simple purposive system is one that is designed to perform a certain set of actions. A complex purposive system is composed of a number of simple purposive systems.[1] An integrated oil company is a complex purposive system designed to explore for hydrocarbon products and to produce, transport, refine and market them. The relatively simple constituents of such a system are the units designed to perform certain functions. Unless the whole system is viable, the specific objectives for which it is designed to perform can not be fulfilled. It is an analogue of human behavior; one which resembles biological organisms. Why not? An organization is substantially an assemblage of people within a certain environment. In this sense an organization is homeostatic; its essential variables are held at desired levels through self-regulation within a complex information-processing and decision-oriented system. Its self-regulations are invariably motivated by its dominating desire to continue doing what it is supposed to do at a certain standard level or set of levels. Unless it survives within a certain frame of reference, the system disintegrates and disappears, an unhappy state of affairs which most biological organisms try to avoid. As such it encompasses the criteria on which their self-regulation is based.

14.3. Income and Its Determination

In a homeostatic model, a set of essential variables is kept within desirable survival levels through the decision-making mechanism of the model. One of these essential variables is income. The level of desirability for this variable is affected by several disturbances arising from the environment of the organization. In other words, the value of one of the essential variables depends upon the environmental variables; whereas, the survival of the

---

1. *Op. cit.*, Chapter 5.

organization depends upon the value that income may take at a certain point in time, other things being equal.

Hence, the range of values that income may take must be kept at a survival level. The determination of this level or desirable value is then a critical question. What is a most desirable level to satisfy a certain pressure group within the environment of the organization is, under certain defined conditions, unsatisfactory to some other pressure groups in the same environment. It is an occasion of conflicting interests. To satisfy conflicting interests is generally impossible by reason of the existence of the conflict unless income takes one value that is more satisfactory than others by comparison within a certain frame of reference.

The neutrality of a judge is the prime assurance for two or more parties to ask for his ruling on an issue characterized by conflicting interests. He is the neutral adjudicator or arbiter. His ruling within an interpretation of a certain frame of reference of a given law or contract is supposedly unbiased and impartial. Hence, by definition, it is satisfactory even to the loser of the case. The frame of reference in our case does not have to be legal. It is sufficient for it to be generally logical and acceptable. This is why the philosophy underlying the determination of survival income level is drawn from conventional and generally acceptable theories and definitions in several fields of knowledge. Such fields include the logic of the sciences and the theories and techniques of organization, cybernetics, accounting, economics, and mathematics. The selection of income determination techniques in light of these premises is then felt to give an unbiased and neutral answer. Hence, by definition, this neutral value satisfies the proposed conflicting interests being as such a satisfactory level for survival. This is experienced in the accounting theory of the neutral value of net income in a somewhat different form.

14.4. Related Research Extension

In the process of handling the income determination question, we had to drop out several other questions directly related to the problem under investigation or to its constituents. Here are some of these questions.

14.4. A. Model Construction and Application for Business Organizations

The organization model we have constructed and applied to the petroleum industry within the context of an accounting question is nothing but an operational one designed to serve a specific purpose. In the way it was presented and applied, it is not a general organization model. Nevertheless, it has the potential of developing into a general one. This further development seems to be feasible within the existing sphere of literature on cybernetics, operations research, contemporary theories of organization, and other business administration fields.

14.4.B *Accounting Reports and Disclosure*

In the process of the limited application of the organization model to the international petroleum industry in Chapter IV, we stated that accounting reports could serve managerial and organizational purposes better if they were more objectively oriented towards environmental disturbances. This is not to say that present managerial accounting reports pay absolutely no attention to such disturbances. The inference is that dynamic business organizations need more of it and can get it by utilizing better analytical tools. Hence, the question of what the form and content of these reports should be, together with the frequency of presentation to management, within the proposed model, is another question for further research. The emphasis on accounting as an integral part of the information-communication network of the model seems to be the obvious point of departure.

Similarly, the form and content of financial information to be disclosed to those outside the organization could also be more purposive than its present state, still within the context of the model.

14.4.C. *Recognition and Measurement Problems for Other Industries*

We have already quoted Sprouse and Moonitz[1] to the effect that business concerns are becoming exceedingly complex so that a formulation of more specific techniques beyond the broad principles of accounting themselves is needed. The authors may not have in mind more specific techniques for specific industries. Nevertheless, the conclusion we have arrived at as a result of this study seems to be in that direction, unless similar studies of other "significant" industries come out with a set of income determining techniques substantially similar to those arrived at in this study. This is at

---

1. Sprouse and Moonitz, *op. cit.*, p. 1.

least one way of approaching the question of devising a universal set of more specific income determination techniques. Should such a study or series of studies be made, the outcome could be useful in two ways. First, the chosen techniques for another industry might provide one or more alternative income determination techniques which could be more objectively used in the international petroleum industry and substituted for one or more of the techniques chosen in this study if this could be done without violating our basic frame of reference. Secondly, such a series of studies could reveal substantial resemblances among the techniques chosen for the international oil industry and those that are the outcome of other studies. These conclusions could then serve as a basis for enlarging whatever present set or sets of accounting principles are available and making them relatively more universal.

14.4.D. Towards Absolute Objectivity and Neutrality

Whether objectivity and neutrality, in the sense of absolutely exact, accurate and truthful accounting measurements could ever be achieved is an open question. We have established a certain frame of reference for our conclusions. Others could and most probably would establish a different one. They might emerge with different conclusions or with substantially similar ones. In the first case, the necessity for further investigation of these questions is apparent. In the second one, we have probably come one step closer towards the absolute truth and neutrality in accounting determinations. We would always strive to come closer than we ever did before.

A Lesson in the Chemistry Of Hydrocarbons

In the definition of atomic theory in *The Handbook of Chemistry and Physics*, it is stated:

> All elementary forms of matter are composed of very small unit quantities called atoms. The atoms of a given element all have the same size and weight. The atoms of different elements have different sizes and weights. Atoms of the same or different elements unite with each other to form very small unit quantities of compound substances called molecules.[1]

The Handbook defines the atom as:

> The smallest part of an element which can participate in ordinary chemical changes. The atoms of a given element are unvarying in average mass, but are different in such mass from atoms of all elements.[2]

Naturally these two definitions apply to petroleum and natural gas in their crude form. The molecules of these chemical compounds are composed mainly of two elements, hydrogen and carbon, and hence they are named hydrocarbons. The hydrocarbon molecules range from very small ones such as methane which contains one carbon atom and four hydrogen atoms (CH_4) to very large ones such as hectacontane which contains 100 carbon

---

1. Charles David Hodgman, *Handbook of Chemistry and Physics* (New York: Chemical Rubber Publishing Co., 1960).
2. *Ibid.*

atoms and 202 hydrogen atoms. The names of these hydrocarbon members are listed in Table A1.[1]

Table A1

Names of the Members of the Hydrocarbons Family

Serial number	Number of C (carbon atoms)	Name of the compound	Serial number	Number of C (carbon atoms)	Name of the compound
1	1	Methane	16	16	Hexadecane
2	2	Ethane	17	17	Heptadecane
3	3	Propane	18	18	Octadecane
4	4	Butane	19	19	Novadecane
5	5	Pentane	20	20	Eicosane
6	6	Hexane	21	21	Heneicosane
7	7	Heptane	22	22	Docosane
8	8	Octane	23	23	Tricosane
9	9	Novane	24	30	Triacontane
10	10	Decane	25	31	Hentriacontane
11	11	Hendecane	26	32	Dotriacontane
12	12	Dodecane	27	33	Tritriacontane
13	13	Tridecane	28	40	Tetracontane
14	14	Tetradecane	29	60	Hexacontane
15	15	Pentadecane	30	100	Hectacontane

Figure A1

Paraffins

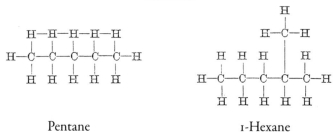

Pentane   1-Hexane

---

1. G. Bryant Bachman, *Organic Chemistry* (New York: McGraw-Hill, 1949), p. 15.

Figure A1 (cont.)

OLEFINS

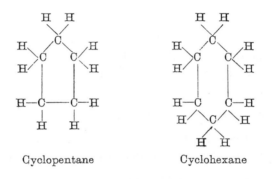

Pentene

Ischexene

NAPHTHENES

Cyclopentane

Cyclohexane

AROMATICS

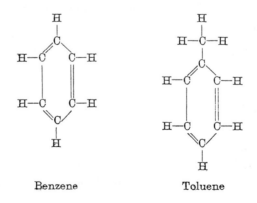

Benzene

Toluene

Fig. A1. Structural diagrams of representative hydrocarbons
(Ras Tannura Oil Operations Manual, Aramco, Dhahran 1956, Fig. 1–1)

The hydrocarbons can be separated into the parts listed in Table A1 according to their boiling points. Natural gas is usually composed of some or all of the first seven compounds. However, the petroleum matter, though primarily composed of carbon and hydrogen atoms, contains some other elements considered as impurities. Sulfur, oxygen, nitrogen, chlorine are some of these impurities. Other constituents of the petroleum matter are water, salt, and some metals. But the main components of the petroleum are carbon and hydrogen, and the absence of any of the impurities does not affect, in any way, the basic structure of the compound. A look into Fig. A1 will reveal that the main chemical characteristic of the hydrocarbons is the presence of carbon and hydrogen.

One of the important classifications of hydrocarbon compounds is the following:

1. *The Paraffins.* Those hydrocarbon compounds which are incapable of uniting with hydrogen. They are termed "saturated" because of this characteristic.[1] The paraffins possess the general formula C_nH_{2n+2} for the determination of the carbon and hydrogen atoms in one molecule of the compound.

2. *The Olefins.* The hydrocarbons which possess the general formula C_nH_{2n} for the determination of the carbon and hydrogen atoms in one molecule of the compound.[2]

3. *The Cycloparaffins.* The hydrocarbon compounds isomeric with the olefins. They also possess the general formula C_nH_{2n}.[3]

4. *The Fourth Category* (The Acetylenes). The classification of hydrocarbons possessing the general formula C_nH_{2n-2}.[4]

The Unsaturated Hydrocarbons

The last three categories of the above-mentioned classification are termed "unsaturated" because of their ability to unite with other elements.

Looking again to Fig. A1, we find that some of the compounds possess a double bond between some of the atoms expressed diagrammatically by two dashes between some of the atoms. Those compounds are named after

---

1. Julius Schmidt, *A Textbook of Organic Chemistry* (London: Gurney and Jackson, 1926).
2. *Ibid.*, p. 117.
3. *Ibid.*
4. *Ibid.*, p. 124.

CHART A1

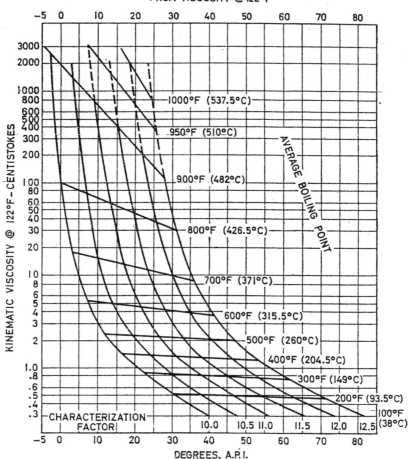

CHARACTERIZATION FACTOR
FROM VISCOSITY @ 122°F

SOURCE:—
K.M. WATSON, E.F. NELSON AND GEORGE B. MURPHY
CHARACTERIZATION OF PETROLEUM FRACTIONS,
INDUSTRIAL AND ENGINEERING CHEMISTRY VOL. 27.
DECEMBER 1935, PAGE 1461 FIG. 3

CHART A2

MOLECULAR WEIGHTS, CRITICAL TEMPERATURES AND CHARACTERIZATION FACTORS OF PETROLEUM FRACTIONS

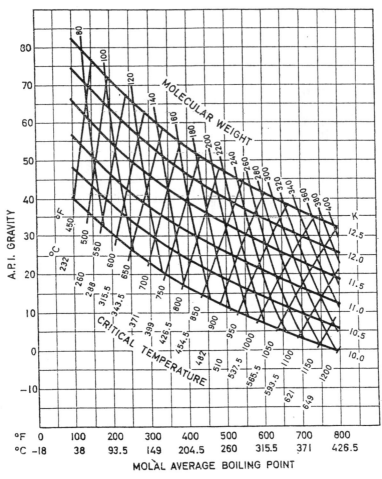

SOURCE:—
K.M. WATSON, E. F. NELSON, AND GEORGE B. MURPHY,
CHARACTERIZATION OF PETROLEUM FRACTIONS,
INDUSTRIAL AND ENGINEERING CHEMISTRY, VOL. 27.
DECEMBER 1935, PAGE 1461 FIG. 1

the corresponding saturated compounds listed in Table A1 by changing the parafix (termination) -ane into -ylane or -ene.[1]

Definitions of the terms in Figure A1

1. *Hydrocarbon* is a chemical composed of atoms of carbon and hydrogen.

2. *Paraffin* is an open-chain hydrocarbon, which is saturated with respect to hydrogen.

3. *Olefin* is a class of open-chain hydrocarbons which are deficient or unsaturated with respect to hydrogen.

4. *Isomere* are chemical compounds having the same composition but different arrangements of the atoms in the molecular structures.

5. *Aromatic hydrocarbons* are characterized by the presence of one or more benzene rings in their structures.

6. *Naphthene* is a class of cyclic or ring hydrocarbons which are saturated with respect to hydrogen.

(*Ras Tannura Oil Operations Manual*, Published by Aramco Training Department, Dhahran, Saudi Arabia, 1956, Glossary pp. i–xv).

---

1. *Ibid.,* p. 117

Technical Data Underlying the Atom-Mol Joint Cost Allocation Methods

The atom-mol methods introduced in Chapter X are based on the technical data presented hereafter. Such data are supplied by the Universal Oil Products Company.

1. Calculation of Weight, Mols and Molecular Weights for Gas

Assume:

A. 500 SCF of gas associated with one barrel of 38° API crude,
B. Gas composition by volume is 40% methane, 25% ethane, 20% propane, and 15% butane.

Then the following calculations are derived. (See table below)

Wt. of 500 SCF gas

$$500 \text{ SCF} \times \frac{1 \text{ lb mol}}{379 \text{ SCF}} \times \frac{31.4 \text{ lb}}{1 \text{ lb mol}} = 41.5 \text{ lb}$$

Wt. of methane

$$500 \text{ SCF gas} \times \frac{40 \text{ SCF methane}}{100 \text{ SCF gas}} \times \frac{1 \text{ lb mol}}{379 \text{ SCF}} \times \frac{16 \text{ lb}}{1 \text{ lb mol}} = 8.5 \text{ lb}$$

Component	Mol %* or vol. %	Mol	MW	lb for 100 mol of gas
Methane	40	40	16	640
Ethane	25	25	30	750

Component	Mol %* or vol. %	Mol	MW	lb for 100 mol of gas
Propane	20	20	44	880
Butane	15	15	58	870
Total	100	100		3140

* Since 1 lb mol is always equivalent to 379 SCF gas and vol. % = mol. %[1]

$$\text{Gas molecular wt.} = \frac{\text{lb}}{\text{mol}} = \frac{3140}{100} = 31.4$$

Wt. of ethane

$$500 \text{ SCF gas} \times \frac{25 \text{ SCF ethane}}{100 \text{ SCF gas}} \times \frac{1 \text{ lb mol}}{379 \text{ SCF}} \times \frac{30 \text{ lb}}{1 \text{ lb mol}} = 9.9 \text{ lb}$$

Wt. of propane

$$500 \text{ SCF gas} \times \frac{20 \text{ SCF propane}}{100 \text{ SCF gas}} \times \frac{1 \text{ lb mol}}{379 \text{ SCF}} \times \frac{44 \text{ lb}}{1 \text{ lb mol}} = 11.9 \text{ lb}$$

Wt. of butane

$$500 \text{ SCF gas} \times \frac{15 \text{ SCF butane}}{100 \text{ SCF gas}} \times \frac{1 \text{ lb mol}}{379 \text{ SCF}} \times \frac{58 \text{ lb}}{1 \text{ lb mol}} = 11.5 \text{ lb}$$

Total: = 41.8 lb

2. Calculation of the Carbon Atoms

If crude is assumed to be comprised of formula C_nH_{2n+2}

Then $12_{(n)+2n+2}$ $= 265$

14_n $= 263$

n $= 18.78$

or 19 carbon atoms

Note: The formula C_nH_{n+2} is not correct for crude oil since the paraffin, naphthene, aromatic composition changes as follows for Arabian crude.[2]

Formulae		390°F end pt.	390–525°F	26.5 API heavy gas oil	23.9 API heavy gas oil
C_nH_{2n+2}	P	65	}79	}56	}51
C_nH_{2n}	N	14			
C_nH_n	A	21	21	44	49

1. W. L. Badger and W. L. McCabe, *Elements of Chemical Engineering* (New York: McGraw-Hill, 1936), p. 8.
2. John Groswold, *Fuel, Combustion and Furnaces*, Chemical Engineering Series (New York: McGraw-Hill, 1936).

Number of carbon atoms if we use formulae:

$$\frac{C_nH_{2n}}{C_{n+2n}} = 265 \qquad\qquad \frac{C_nH_n}{C_nH_n} = 265$$

$$12_{n+2n} = 265 \qquad\qquad 12_{2n+n} = 265$$

$$14_n = 265 \qquad\qquad 13_n = 265$$

$$n = 18.93 \qquad\qquad n = 20.01$$

Note: A number of 19 carbon atoms is taken to be a representative number for accounting purposes.

3. Calculation of Molecular Weight for Crude Oil

For 1 bbl of 36° API Crude[1]

$$°API = \frac{141.5}{d\frac{60}{60}} - 131.5$$

$$d\frac{60}{60} = 0.844 \quad \text{where} \quad d\frac{60}{60} \text{ is specific gravity}$$

Or

$$1 \text{ bbl crude} \times 0.844\frac{(8.33)\text{ lb}}{\text{gal}} \times \frac{42\text{ gal}}{1\text{ bbl}} = 249\text{ lb}$$

$$1 \text{ bbl crude} \times \frac{5.62\text{ CF}}{\text{bbl}} \times 0.844\frac{(62.4)}{\text{CF}} = 294\text{ lb}$$

crude oil viscosity 43.4[3] SSU @ 110°F

43.4 SSU @ 100°F = 5.4 centistokes @ 100°F (see Chart A1)

from Chart 1

average boiling point = 600°F

characterization factor = 12.1

from Chart A2

molecular weight = 265

4. Calculation of Carbon Atom-Mol Method

	C_i carbon atoms	w_i quantity lb	(MW_i) mol. wt.	M_i^* mol	C_iM_i
Methane	1	8.5	16	0.531	0.531

---

1. California Research Corporation Manual, 1957.

	C_i carbon atoms	w_i quantity lb	(MW_i) mol. wt.	M_i^* mol	C_iM_i
Ethane	2	9.9	30	0.330	0.660
Propane	3	11.9	44	0.370	0.810
Butane	4	11.5	58	0.198	0.792
Crude oil	19	294.0	265	1.110	21.100
				2.439	23.893

$$* M_i = \frac{w_i}{MW_i}$$

$$\text{Cost formula} = \frac{C_iM_i}{\displaystyle\sum_1^n C_iM_i} \times 100$$

$$\text{Gas cost} = \frac{2.793}{23.893} \times 100 = 11.7\%$$

$$\text{Crude cost} = \frac{21.100}{23.893} \times 100 = 88.3\%$$

5. Calculation of the Hydrogen Atom-Mol Method

	h_i carbon atoms	w_i quantity lb	(MW_i) mol. wt.	M_i^* mol	h_iM_i
Methane	4	8.5	16	0.531	2.124
Ethane	6	9.9	30	0.330	1.980
Propane	8	11.9	44	0.270	2.160
Butane	10	11.5	58	0.198	1.980
Crude oil	40	294.0	265	1.110	44.400
					52.644

$$\text{Cost formula} = \frac{h_iM_i}{\displaystyle\sum_1^n h_iM_i} \times 100$$

$$\text{Gas cost} = \frac{8.244}{52.644} \times 100 = 15.7\%$$

$$\text{Crude cost} = \frac{44.40}{52.644} \times 100 = 84.3\%$$

Bibliography

Accounting Research Bulletin 43, American Institute of Certified Public Accountants, New York, 1953.

ADELMAN, M. A., *The Supply and Price of Natural Gas*, Basil Blackwell, Oxford, 1962.

AL-KHODARI, FATHI, "The 50–50 Formula under the Financial Legislation and Accounting Principles followed by Petroleum Companies in the Middle East", Third Arab Petroleum Congress, Alexandria, October 16–21, 1961. Translation from Arabic original made by A. H. Taher.

AL-TARIKI, ABDULLA, "Arab Oil", a lecture delivered before the Iraqi Engineers Association, Baghdad, June 1, 1963. Arabic and English versions of the lecture are by Al-Tariki.

American Accounting Association, *Accounting and Reporting Standards for Corporate Financial Statements and Preceding Statement and Supplements*, Columbus, Ohio, 1957.

American Institute of Certified Public Accountants, *Accounting Terminology Bulletin* No.1, "Review and resume", New York, 1953.

ASHBY, WILLIAM ROSS, An Introduction to Cybernetics, John Wiley, New York, 1957.

AYER, A. J., *et al., Studies in Communication*, contributions by A. J. Ayer, J. B. S. Haldane, Colin Cherry, Sir Geoffrey Vickers, J. Z. Young, R. Wittkower, T .B. L. Webster, Randolph Quirk, and D. B. Fry, with an introduction by B. Ifor Evans; Martin Secker and Warburg, London, 1955.

BACHMAN, G. BRYANT, *Organic Chemistry*, First Edition, McGraw-Hill, New York, 1949.

BACKER, MORTON, editor, *Handbook of Accounting Theory*, Prentice-Hall, New York, 1955.

BADGER. W. L., and McCABE, Elements of Chemical Engineering, McGraw-Hill, New York and London 1936.

BAIN, JOE S., *The Economics of the Pacific Coast Petroleum Industry, Part I*, The University of California Press, Berkeley and Los Angeles, 1944.

BEER, STAFFORD, *Cybernetics and Management*, The English Universities Press, London, 1960.

BES, J., *Tanker Shipping*, Drukkerij J./H. C. DeBoer Jr., Hilversum (Netherlands), 1963.

CHANDLER, L. E., and BELTAGI, B. E., "Auditing and its Role in the Middle East Oil Industry", unpublished paper, Arabian American Oil Company, Dhahran, Saudi Arabia, 1961.

Chase Manhattan Bank, *Annual Analysis of the Petroleum Industry*, Petroleum Department, The Chase Manhattan Bank, New York, 1958–1962.

Chase Manhattan Bank, *Future Growth of the World Petroleum Industry*, Petroleum Department, The Chase Manhattan Bank, New York, September, 1961.

EDDISON, R. T., PENNYCUICK, K., and RIVETT, H. H. P., *Operational Research in Management*, The English Universities Press, London, 1962.

GRISWOLD, JOHN, *Fuel, Combustion and Furnaces*, Chemical Engineering Series, McGraw-Hill, 1936.

HARBISON, FREDERICK, and MYERS, CHARLES, *Management in the Industrial World*, An International Analysis, McGraw-Hill, 1959.

HARRE, R., *An Introduction to the Logic of the Sciences*, Macmillan, London, 1960.

HARTSHORN, J. E., *Oil Companies and Governments*, Faber and Faber, London, 1962.

HODGMAN, CHARLES DAVID, *Handbook of Chemistry and Physics*, Chemical Rubber Publishing Company, New York, 1960.'

ISSAWI, CHARLES, and YEGANEH, MOHAMMED, *The Economics of Middle Eastern Oil*, Faber and Faber, London 1962.

LASKI, J. G., "A Route to Better Management Control", The Sixth World Petroleum Congress, Frankfurt/Main, 19–26 June, 1963.

LEBKICHER, ROY, RENTZ, GEORGE, and STEINEKE, MAX, *Aramco Handbook*, Arabian American Oil Company, Dhahran, Saudi Arabia, 1960.

LEEMAN, WAYNE A., *The Price of Middle East Oil*, Cornell University Press, Ithaca, New York, 1962.

LENCZOWSKI, GEORGE, *Oil and State in the Middle East*, Cornell University Press, Ithaca, New York, 1960.

LEWIS, W. A. "Overhead costs", *Some Essays in Economic Analysis*, George Allen and Unwin, Ltd, London 1959.

LITTLETON, A. C., and YAMEY, B. S. *Studies in the History of Accounting*, Richard D. Irwin, Homewood, Ill., 1957.

LUCE, R. DUNCAN, and RAIFFA, HOWARD, *Games and Decisions*, John Wiley, New York, 1957.

MARCH, JAMES, G., and SIMON, HERBERT A., *Organizations*, John Wiley, New York, 1957.

MOONITZ, MAURICE, *The Basic Postulates of Accounting*, American Institute of CPAs, New York, 1961.

MOONITZ, MAURICE, *The Entity Theory of Consolidated Statements*, The Foundation Press, Brooklyn, 1951.

NEWMAN, JAMES, R., editor, *What is Science?*, Washington Square Press, New York, 1961.

Organization of Petroleum Exporting Countries, (OPEC), *Radical Changes in the International Oil Industry During the Past Decade*, IVth Arab Petroleum Congress, Beirut, November 5–12, 1963.

OPEC, *Explanatory Memoranda on the OPEC Resolution*, Geneva, July, 1962.

OPEC, *The Price of Crude Oil, A Rational Approach*, IVth Arab Petroleum Congress, Beirut, November 5–12, 1963.

PATON, W. A., and LITTLETON, A. C., *An Introduction to Corporate Accounting Standards*, American Accounting Association, Columbus, Ohio, 1956.

PORTER, S. P., *Determining the Cost of Finding and Producing Gas Under Federal Power Commission Regulation*, American Petroleum Institute Publication, Vol. 38 (vii), 1958.

PRYOR, F. X., *Uniform System of Accounts for Concession Oil Companies in the Middle East*, Committee of Petroleum Exports, Jeddah. 1959. (unpublished)

Ras Tannura Oil Operations Manual, Arabian American Oil Company, Dhahran, Saudi Arabia, 1956.

RATHBONE, MONROE J., "Oil in the Service of Man", Sixth World Petroleum Congress, Frankfurt/Main, June 1963.

SCHMIDT, JULIUS, *A Textbook of Organic Chemistry*, English Edition by H. Gordon Rule, Gurney and Jackson, London, 1926.

SHANNON, CLAUDE E., and WEAVER, WARREN, *The Mathematical Theory of Communication*, University of Illinois Press, Urbana, 1949.

SIMON, HERBERT A., *Models of Man, Social and Rational*, John Wiley, New York, 1957.

SMITH, C. AUBREY, and BROCK, HORACE R., *Accounting for Oil and Gas Producers*, Prentice Hall, Englewood Cliff, 1959.

SPROUSE, ROBERT T., and MOONITZ, MAURICE, *A Tentative Set of Broad Accounting Principles for Business Enterprises*, American Institute of CPAs, New York, 1962.

Study Group on Business Income, *Five Monographs on Business Income, American Institute of Accountants*, New York, 1950.

TAHER, A. H., *Cost Accounting as a Means of Managerial and Financial*

Control of the Petroleum Industry, 3rd Arab Petroleum Congress, Alexandria, October 16–21, 1962.

TERRY, GEORGE R., *Principles of Management*, Richard D. Irwin, Inc. Homewood, Ill., 1956.

THOMAS, WILLIAM, E., *Readings in Cost Accounting*, South Western Publishing Co. Cincinnati, Ohio, 1960.

URNER, SAMUEL E., and ORANGE, WILLIAM B., *Elements of Mathematical Analysis*, Ginn and Company, Boston, 1950.

U.S. Internal Revenue Code, Sections 613 (a) and 613 (b), 1960.

U.S. Treasury, Regulation 118, Section 39, 23 (m)–16 (a) (1).

VATTER, WILLIAM J., *The Fund Theory of Accounting and its Implications for Financial Reports*, The University of Chicago Press, 1947.

WALLER, ROBERT E., *Oil Accounting*, University of Toronto Press, Canada, 1957.

WALLS, M. J., *The Oil Industry Tomorrow*, Report of the Summer Meeting of the Institute of Petroleum, the Institute of Petroleum, London, 1962.

WIENER, NORBERT, *The Human Use of Human-Beings, Cybernetics and Society*, Houghton Mifflin, Boston, 1954.

WIXON, RUFUS, and KELL, WALTER G., *Accountant's Handbook*, The Ronald Press, New York, 1957.

Journals and Periodicals

Al-Bilad Daily Newspaper, July 14, 1963, Translation by A. H. Taher.

Business Week, McGraw-Hill, New York, August 6, 1960.

The Economist, June 29, 1963.

Industrial and Engineering Chemistry, The American Chemical Society.

Journal of Accountancy, July, 1947, "The case against administrative expense in inventory", Jonathan Harris.

Petroleum Intelligence Weekly, Petroleum Intelligence, New York, September 2, 1963.

Index